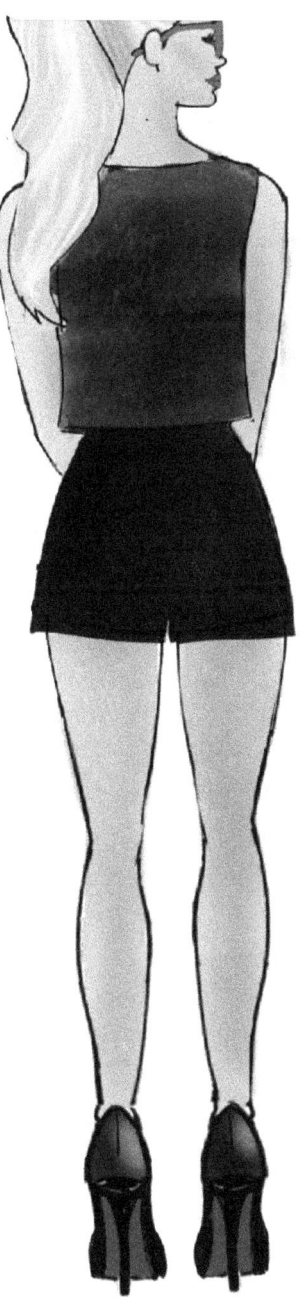

An ode to modern millennial dating.

# No Pay May

*thirty one dates in thirty one days*

A story by
Extra Cash Cathy

Copyright © 2018 Extra Cash Cathy

All rights reserved. No part of this publication may be reproduced, distributed, or transmitted in any form or by any means, including photocopying, recording, or other electronic or mechanical methods, without the prior written permission of the publisher, except in the case of brief quotations embodied in critical reviews and certain other noncommercial uses permitted by copyright law.

ISBN-13: 978-1-945532-75-7
Library of Congress Control Number: 2018941145

Published by Opportune Independent Publishing Co.
For permission requests, write to the publisher, addressed "Attention: Permissions Coordinator" to the address below.

Info@opportunepublishing.com
113 N. Live Oak Street
Houston, TX 77003

Cover Illustration by Chelsea Lundy
Digital Artist & Owner ©Chelsdrawsyou
Located at www.chelsdrawsyou.com

Cover Design in collaboration with Alissa KR Goltzman
Located at www.akrgraphics.com

Contact Cathy - www.nopaymay.com @nopaymaybook

Dedicated to my father, who will probably never read this diary of my dating life.

# TABLE OF CONTENTS

## Prologue
- Foundation — 11
- Rules — 13
- Operation No Pay May: Underway — 15

## Week One
- Date Diary: Quiet but Not Shy — 21
- Date Diary: Over Talker — 25
- Date Diary: Cynical Dater — 29
- Date Diary: The Transient — 33
- Date Diary: Preppy Texter — 37
- Date Diary: Too Good to be True — 41
- Date Diary: Brunch Enthusiast — 45
- Date Diary: PFG & Short Shorts — 49
- Date Diagnosis — 53

## Week Two
- Date Diary: Perfect Dater — 57
- Date Diary: Metro Man — 61
- Date Diary: Cheap Ass — 65
- Date Diary: Foul Mouth — 69
- Date Diary: Derby Dude — 73
- Date Diary: Adjuster — 77
- Date Diagnosis — 79

## Week Three
- Date Diary: Hint Dropper — 83
- Date Diary: Future Boyfriend — 87
- Date Diary: Brussels Sprouts — 91
- Date Diary: Sweet Intentions — 95
- Date Diary: Bird Poop — 99
- Date Diary: Donut Hole — 103
- Date Diary: Foul Mouth – Part Two — 107
- Date Diagnosis — 109

## Week Four
- Date Diary: Suit & Tie — 113
- Date Diary: Big Personality — 119
- Date Diary: Banana Republic — 123
- Date Diary: Anal Bandit — 127
- Date Diary: Kiss Cam — 131
- Date Diary: Suit & Tie – Part Two — 135
- Date Diary: Tinted Oakley's — 139
- Date Diary: Creepy MF — 143
- Date Diary: Borderline Rapist — 147
- Date Diary: DJ Blenz — 153

## Epilogue
- Date Diary Recap — 159
- The End of No Pay May — 165

## Appendix

# PROLOGUE

Technology has never been more prevalent in our society. Technology has never been more prevalent in my dating life. I can meet anyone, anywhere, anytime. In May of 2016, I set out on a mission to explore modern dating. And boy, I experienced it. All at once. Dove in head first.

This is that story. The diary of my dating life. The diary of a girl full of love and laughter experiencing modern dating for the first time. The diary of a girl learning that her traditional background has no place in the world of modern dating.

The story starts with an idea, a pure foundation built on one question; is it possible to go on a date every night? This story is how I, a 24-year-old millennial woman raised in the south, answered the question.

Through my experience, I learned modern dating changes our ideas of love, sex, dating, and the way we interact with strangers. As the comedian Aziz Ansari points out in his book Modern Romance, the way people meet and seek love has radically changed from community-based, value-centric unions. He believes online daters are slowly becoming cheap hookers. I believe online dating causes overstimulation and disconnection, often diminishing the dream of romance. Online dating is nothing more than a daunting job search.

You may notice that each date dairy follows a specific format. This format allowed me to compare every date with the others. I kept every person involved in No Pay May anonymous, including myself... until now. My thoughts are written as I experienced them. The events are written as they played out in real time.

No time to waste. Please enjoy my own personal ode to modern millennial dating featuring Tinder, Bumble, Coffee Meets Bagel, Hinge, Twitter, and my local radio station.

# No Pay May

*thirty one dates in thirty one days*

# FOUNDATION

April 18, 2016

      Two weeks ago, I was Face Timing a college friend and told her about my dating life.

      Apparently, I've peaked at the young age of 24, or suddenly men started getting REAL about relationships. Either way, my dating life picked up. Boys from bars, boys from work, and even boys I'm "just friends" with began asking me out. It seemed like I jumped into this "dating phase" of my life overnight. Each date I went on was different from the others, except for one commonality… dinner! As I rambled to my friend about all the free food I was getting, my friend paused and said, "Imagine how many dates you would get if you were online dating?". Over a few late-night phone calls and some creativity, Operation: *No Pay May* was birthed.

      The basis of Operation: *No Pay May* is a social dating experiment. Currently our society is confused on what "dating" means. Everyone seems to have their own view on when a date is a date. Girls think guys just want to "hook up", and boys think girls want relationships in which couples spend every second together. After talking to many friends, I found neither of these is true. As females, we categorize all men, and men seem to do the same. The truth is nobody fits into these overgeneralizations. To determine what you want and who you are, you need to "date" different types of people. How are you going to do this if you don't put yourself out there? I've decided to become an open-minded dater in pursuit of answers.

The goal is to go on 31 dates in 31 consecutive days. Yes, a date (and potentially a free meal) every day for an entire month. Can it be done? I'll document every date using my own Date Diary. I'm assuming I will go on a few bad dates and a few good dates. Other than that, I'm here to learn.

Godspeed,
Extra Cash Cathy

# RULES

On these dates, I cannot:

1. Pay (I can offer, but, if I pay I cannot count it as a date)
2. Lie about myself
3. ~~Count the date if I do not receive any form of free food~~
    *see week one's Date Diagnosis
4. Date any Deal Breakers
    - Guys who are younger than 24 and older than 32
    - Guys with kids
    - Guys looking for one night stands
    - Guys under 5'10
5. Date any boys I've previously dated
6. Initiate a second date
7. Use guy friends to fill in gap days or last-minute cancels
8. Tell my dates about Operation: *No Pay May*

# OPERATION: NO PAY MAY GETS UNDERWAY

April 23, 2016

     The initial plan was to begin Operation: *No Pay May* on May 1, 2016. Due to unexpected situations, my first date will be on April 24, 2016. Let me explain…

     I downloaded six different dating apps in the span of six days. On Monday, April 18, 2016, Houston was hit with a flash flood. It left many Houstonians with damaged houses, flooded cars, and no work. This is the day I decided to download four dating apps. What else are you supposed to do when you're stuck in your house with a bottle of wine and a pending mission? Because I know nothing about dating apps or online dating, I clearly jumped the gun by downloading these apps two weeks ahead of schedule. The day after I downloaded these apps, boys were asking me out. I quickly learned that boys don't want to wait two weeks to meet up. By the end of the week, I had a date set up for Sunday, Monday, Tuesday, and Wednesday. I figured Operation: *No Pay May* might as well start in April. Below is a diagnosis of each app I downloaded.

### Dating App Diagnosis

**Tinder** – Downloaded Monday, April 18, 2016. From a social perspective, Tinder's reputation is negative. Most of my friends believe Tinder is only for hook ups. After a week of swiping right, I have 50 matches and 3 planned dates. On

Tinder, I do none of the initial texts, and I don't have to. Out of the 50 matches, 20 of them message me first, and three initiate plans.

**Bumble** – Downloaded Monday, April 18, 2016. Word on the street is Bumble is the dating app. Apparently, girls having to message boys first translates into dates, not hookups. Bumble is WORK. I have to initiate a conversation within 24 hours or the matches disappear. I match 8 boys in one night and must message them all within 24 hours. What girl has time for that? It's exhausting. Boys seem to be more into messaging than meeting up on Bumble. The 10 boys I messaged never initiated plans.

**Coffee Meets Bagel** – Downloaded Monday, April 18, 2016. At the end of week one, Coffee Meets Bagel won me over. It's simple. You get five "bagels" to choose from every day (profiles). If you both like each other, you have a week to start a conversation. From my experience, the Coffee Meets Bagel boys are looking for relationships. I have had fewer matches and fewer messages, but more dates than from any other app.

**Happn** – Downloaded Monday, April 18, 2016. Happn is a GPS dating app. Profiles show up on your feed if you physically cross paths with that person. It's a little creepy. I'm not a fan. Tinder, Bumble, and Coffee Meets Bagel force you to focus on one profile at a time, but Happn does not. Throughout the week, I use Happn only a handful of times. At the end of the week, I am messaging two guys.

**Ok Cupid** – Downloaded Saturday, April 23, 2016, due to pure curiosity. My friend mentioned OKC was intended for relationships. Since I'm basically an online dating investigator, I decided to give it a try. MISTAKE. OKC is by far my least favorite. OKC allows anyone (and I mean anyone) to message you. You don't have to view their profile, match with them, or do anything. The problem with this… in one day, I have over 300 likes and 60 messages. Who on this planet has time to go through 300 peoples' profiles and scroll through 60 messages? OKC does allow you to filter for specifics, but those people get lost in between the non consensuals. I will probably never go on a date using OKC and regret ever downloading it.

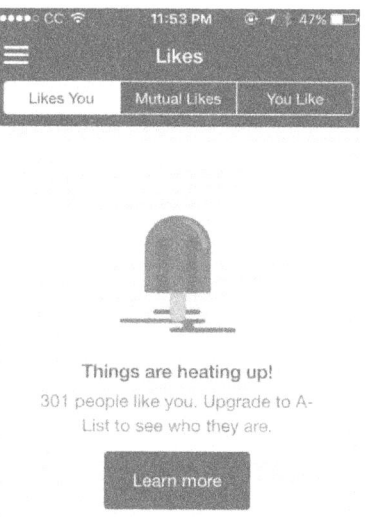

**The Grade** – Downloaded Saturday, April 23, 2016, to spite my OKC experience. The Grade is supposed to be "better quality". You have a say in everything, ie. whom you look at, who can message you, etc. Plus, you're allowed to "grade" each person you match or message with. The grading is supposed to notify other individuals that this person is quality. In theory this could work, but the reality is there are fewer people on the app and fewer people of quality. Since I downloaded it one day ago, nothing has come of it.

**Takeaways**: This is going to be more work than anticipated. Keeping up the matching and messaging long enough for boys to initiate plans is time consuming. I'm messaging boys all day, every day.

# Week One

# DATE DIARY: QUIET BUT NOT SHY

April 25, 2016

**Date's Nickname**: Quiet but not Shy

**Age**: 31

**Occupation**: Resident Doctor

**How We Met**: Tinder. He messages me for three days before asking if we could "hang out in real life?"

**Where We Went**: Food and Drinks–Batanga, a wine and tapas bar downtown

**Second Stop**: Captain Foxheart's, a downtown bar and spirit lodge

**What I Ate**: Vegetarian Tapas–eggplant fries, zucchini tortilla, elotes. Two specialty cocktails.

**Total Estimate**: $43

**Prior Expectations**: I'm excited to meet this guy. Our personalities seem to mesh via text message. He is intelligent and witty. I'm expecting fireworks.

**Date Diary**: I show up before him and wait patiently at the hostess table for him to arrive.

**First Thoughts**: He is tall, looks exactly like his profile picture, and has this cute nerdy thing going on.

I say "Hi," and these words come out of my mouth: "Are we supposed to hug or handshake?"

He gives me a weird side hug before we sit down at our table.

I remember he wrote "quiet but not shy" in his Tinder profile, and it's the truth. We sit down and look over the menu. I tell him I'm a vegetarian, and he ends up ordering for both of us (WHICH I LOVED). We order the same cocktail and start the small talk. During our entire date, we're making references to our text conversations. I ask him about his Tinder dating experiences and tell him about my recent dating app experiences. Yes, I tell him I downloaded lots of dating apps five days ago. I tell him about the trends I see in men's profiles, and he tells me about the trends he sees in women's profiles. I learn so much.

I think this topic of conversation sparks his interest because he says, "Yeah, I was telling my mom about you when I was home for the weekend." I let that sink in.

Basically, his mom asked him if he was dating anyone, and he told her he was going on a date with a girl he met through an app. *Smooth, Doctor, Smooth.* I am flattered that he likes me enough to tell his mom. Side note: I catch him steal a couple of glances at my boobs during dinner. I don't blame him, but he could have be more subtle.

Before the bill comes, Quiet but Not Shy asks if I want to go to a bar down the street. I say yes. He grabs the bill and hands the waiter his card before I have time to offer. We arrive at the empty bar next door. No one is here, just the two of us and the bartenders.

This is where it gets good. We order our second cocktail of the night, which he pays for. He puts his arm around my chair and starts caressing my back. He did this for about two minutes before removing his arm and never touching me again. Maybe he's waiting for me to make a counter move? I was into it, so he didn't have to stop. Quiet but Not Shy tells me he reads sci-fi novels for fun, and I tell him I read religious novels for fun. Shortly after, he gets up to use the restroom, and I sneak a Snapchat picture of the empty bar.

After he returns, he asks if I'm ready to head out. He offers me a ride home and I accept. We walk to his Infinity, and he opens my door before I get in. THIS IS THE FIRST TIME THAT HAS EVER HAPPENED. I love it. We make more small talk on the ride home. I wonder if he'll make a move when he drops me off. He doesn't. I tell him I had a great time and thank him for inviting me out. I get out of the car, and he waits until I make it inside before leaving.

**Takeaways**: Alright, these dates are AWKWARD. Meeting someone for the first time is awkward. You can view someone one way over text message but differently in person. I have no idea what he was thinking. If he wanted to kiss me, he should've said something, or made a move. I'm a firm believer in men initiating dates. Tell me what you want! Communication is the key. Overall, I had a great time with Quiet but Not Shy. I would go out with him again.

# DATE DIARY: OVER TALKER

April 26, 2016

**Date's Nickname**: Over Talker

**Age**: 24

**Occupation**: Med school student

**How We Met**: Coffee Meets Bagel. He asks me on a date right after I replied to the first initial message. This is what I like–straight to the point.

**Where We Went**: Dinner–Fadi's Mediterranean Grill. Drinks–Valhalla, a bar for Rice graduates

**What I Ate**: The falafel platter and a Diet Coke

**Total Cost Estimate**: $12

**Prior Expectations**: This guy likes to ask me in-depth questions over texts and sends novel responses, to which I respond with two sentences, so I expect a non-stop two-hour conversation with very frequent pauses.

**Date Diary:** He waits out front of Fadi's for me to arrive. We side hug and enter the restaurant.

**First Thoughts**: He's fit, shorter than me, total nerd with his shirt tucked in and Nike branded eye glasses. A real people person.

Let me just say that Fadi's is a TERRIBLE place for a first date. First, it's a counter service. We started in line together, but wanted different food options. People ended up in between us in line and I'm panicking thinking "Am I about to pay for my food?" I think he notices the look of panic on my face, and tells me that he is going to pay. Perfect; up front and honest. Fadi's is crowded due to an event. A man speaks from a podium in a partially closed off room to an audience of 20 people. The only empty table in this entire restaurant is a table directly across from the event. Yes, we can hear everything. Yes, we cannot hear each other. Yes, we are asked to keep our voices down. Yes, this is the worst place I've ever been to on a first date.

Thirty minutes later, our food is gone and Over Talker wants to leave. He asks if I want to go to a bar in Rice Village. I agree, and he drives us. From this point forward, there are no awkward pauses.

For a moment during the drive to Valhalla, I start fearing for my life. Over Talker is driving in the opposite direction of Rice Village. As he chats about how the neighborhood we're driving through is experiencing gentrification, I pause and realize…

- The restaurant where we ate is located in Houston's rumored highest activity region for human trafficking.
- I'm in a car with a man I just met online.
- I'm unfamiliar with this route to Rice Village.

Let me reach for my cell phone and call Liam Neeson because I'm about to be Taken.

I'm all for giving people the benefit of the doubt, so I simply say, "I think you are driving in the opposite direction of Rice Village."

Turns out, Over Talker is bad with directions and is driving to Rice Village from memory instead of Google Maps. Strike one.

We park and walk through the campus to Valhalla. I order a Diet Coke because I don't like to drink on weeknights. He mimics my move and goes for a Diet Coke.

Here we go again with the caressing. We take our Diet Cokes on a walk around the campus and stop to sit on a bench. Over Talker talks, and I listen. At one point, he starts caressing my leg during our conversation. I'm a little taken aback by it. Not because I'm not flattered, but I realize right then that I'm not romantically attracted to this guy. Strike two.

Over Talker is also an Over Sharer. On the drive back to my car, I bring up dating apps (it's my current hobby). I ask him if he's been on any bad dates using these apps. He then proceeds to tell me not just about his last few dates, BUT his entire relationship history and exact details; how long they dated, why they broke up, who broke up with whom. Strike three.

We arrive back at Fadi's, where I left my car. We hug and exchange phone numbers. Over Talker texts me later that night asking if I got home safely and if I would like to get dinner again sometime (His text message was as long as this date diary).

**Takeaways**: Over Talker is a great guy. Very friendly and open. However, I don't think I will go out with him again. I would like another dinner, but I know too much about him already. Honestly, I can't see it going anywhere long term. This is now the second guy that initiated a little physical touch but didn't follow through on the kiss. I'm not sure I would've kissed this guy, but it wouldn't have hurt him to try.

# DATE DIARY: CYNICAL DATER

April 27, 2016

**Date's Nickname**: Cynical Dater

**Age**: 26

**Occupation**: Freelance Marketer

**How We Met**: Tinder. He originally asks to "get coffee or go for a walk." Instead, we make plans to grab an early dinner on Tuesday.

**Where We Went**: Dinner–Aka Sushi during happy hour.

**What I Ate**: Edamame and an avocado and cucumber roll.

**Total Cost Estimate**: $10

**Prior Expectations**: I made plans with this guy several days in advance to grab an early dinner, which he agreed to. Every day leading up to our dinner, he asks me to hangout "even if just for 10 minutes." I reject every offer because I have a tight schedule these days. He seems VERY eager and VERY into me.

**Date Diary**: I arrive before him and wait 15 minutes.

**First Thoughts**: He's shorter than me. Too short. I don't think this will work out. Very fit. Dresses well.

Another awkward side hug occurs before we're escorted to our booth. I start telling him about Aka Sushi and how much I love their happy hour. Conversation seems to flow easily. Initial small talk is exchanged before we start talking about deeper subjects. After 10 minutes on this "date," I realize he's a cynical dater. We start discussing dating apps because that seems to be our only common interest. Cynical Dater starts telling me that he hates the term "dating" because he doesn't believe in traditional dating. He says traditional dating is no longer relevant in our society and it often seems like women only "date" to get free meals. I am interested in what he is saying. It's the thesis of this social experiment. Secretly, I'm a little annoyed because I don't think this guy will offer to pay for my meal.

We jump into a good 30-minute conversation about dating, in which the following exchange arises:

Me: "So how do you get to know people if you don't take them on dates?"

Him: "I have my own method. I ask girls if they want to meet in a general setting (i.e. coffee, walk, etc.) before taking them on a date. Usually I can tell within the first 10 minutes if I like her enough to take her on a second date. This way, I don't have to waste my time or money."

Me: "That means when you were asking me to hang out with you even if it was only 10 minutes' every day leading up to our date, you were just trying to decide if I was worth your time or money. That is not at all what I read into that situation. I saw an overeager man trying to get me to do anything I could to meet up with him when we already had set plans. I actually was very put off by that because you seemed too eager."

Him: "Yes, so when you said no, I took the risk and showed up anyways."

He continues to tell me that he's (obviously) never

had a serious relationship. I try to help the poor guy out and explain my perspective: women love to be wanted, even chased. If you're not going to be the guy to spend time and money on them, someone else will. I have so many men asking me out over messages daily. What separates Cynical Dater from the rest? The men who work harder are the ones who succeed. Even then, paying for the first date implies a man is looking for a romantic relationship. If I pay for my own food on the first date, then we are just friends, and there will be no second date.

To be clear, Cynical Dater isn't looking for a "hook up." He wants a relationship but doesn't want to put in the work it takes to build a relationship. Many people want to be in a relationship but are too lazy to put in the time or money. My questions to those people are: How bad do you really want a relationship? Do you even know what kind of relationship you want?

I offer to pay. He declines and does in fact pay for my $10 meal. I'm a cheap date, even for the harshest cynics. He walks me to my car and gives me a hug.

**Takeaways**: I will not be going out with this guy again. I would be friends but nothing more. I did learn from Cynical Dater, which in the end is the ultimate goal.

# DATE DIARY: THE TRANSIENT

April 28, 2016

**Date's Nickname**: The Transient

**Age**: 28
**Occupation**: Regional Sales Manager

**How We Met**: Tinder. I ask him if he wanted to grab dinner or drinks. He responds with drinks.

**Where We Went**: Drinks–Kirby Ice House
Dinner–Local Foods

**What I Ate**: Falafel sandwich

**Total Cost Estimate**: $11

**Prior Expectations**: My worst fear ensues. The guy I am supposed to meet tonight cancels three hours before our scheduled meet up time. Luckily, I've been messaging another guy on Tinder all day.

**Date Diary**: The Transient chose to meet at Kirby Ice House at 7 p.m. I arrive before him, order, and pay for my own drink. He arrives shortly after, orders a drink, and sits outside on the patio.

**First Thoughts**: Cute. A little shorter than me, but not a deal breaker (it's difficult when you're 6'1). Dressed very casual.

Because we started messaging on Tinder that same day, we can still discuss general "about me" questions. I tell him about my job, and he tells me about his. The Transient moved to Houston in December and doesn't have many friends (now I know why he didn't hesitate to say yes to a last-minute meet up). Conversation flows easily, and there are few awkward pauses. The Tinder topic comes up, and he tells me his opinions. The Transient has lived in three different cities in the last two years, so he uses Tinder to meet people in real life. The Transient notices people are more active on Tinder during the early part of the week. For example, he receives more matches and messages on Mondays, Tuesdays, and Wednesdays as opposed to Thursdays, Fridays and Saturdays. Most people have other plans on the weekends.

I start to get hungry and mention the food trucks parked at the bar. Apparently, Wednesday nights are Steak Nights at Kirby (this plays to my advantage). I head to the bar to ask the bartender if anything other than red meat is on the menu. She declines, forcing me to get creative.

I tell The Transient that I am going to grab dinner and ask if he wants to join. He agrees, and I select Local Foods as our next destination. We meet up five minutes later out front of Local Foods. It's a counter service, so I'm thinking the payment situation might be awkward. We order together, and he hands the cashier his card.

I thank him and say, "You didn't have to pay. That was very generous." Secretly, I think, "I can't believe I pulled that off."

I escort him to the outside patio. The longer we sit outside, the more The Transient mentions how much he is enjoying Local Foods. By the end of the date, he's made so many comments about the food, atmosphere, lighting, astro turf, etc. that I start to wonder if he's enjoying Local Foods more than he is enjoying me. I can tell he's becoming more comfortable. At the beginning of our date, The Transient was a little nervous and slipping over words. By the end of the date, I can barely get a word in.

We exchange a hug before leaving, and he says he would "like to do this again sometime."

I agree and walk in the opposite direction to my car. I receive a text message when I get home from The Transient asking if I made it home safely.

**Takeaways**: This has been my favorite date thus far. Much more relaxed than the others. There was no caressing or really any sign of physical touch. It felt like two people hanging out and getting to know each other. But he paid for my meal. This indicates to me that he is looking for more than a friendship, and I'd be into it!

# DATE DIARY: PREPPY TEXTER

April 29, 2016

**Date's Nickname**: Preppy Texter

**Age**: 28

**Occupation**: Lawyer/Federal Judge Clerk

**How We Met**: Tinder. He super likes me and asks to "hang out" anytime this week.

**Where We Went**: Drinks and Dinner–Axelrad and Luigi's Pizzera

**What I Ate**: Two Austin East Ciders and a vegetarian slice of pizza

**Total Cost Estimate**: $8 (because I paid for one cider)

**Prior Expectations**: I don't have many. The "hangout" throws me for a loop. Am I getting dinner? Is it a date? He asks me to wear my glasses when we meet. Guess he's into smart girls?

**Date Diary**: I walk into Axelrad at the exact moment he does. Talk about perfect timing.

**First Thoughts**: He's better looking in person than on Tinder (never thought that would happen). Dressed very preppy with his khakis and boat shoes. A tad bit shorter than me. Preppy Texter orders the first round of drinks. We sit across from each other at a picnic table and start talking about our jobs, background, families, and the usual boring stuff. Conversation flows easily.

Here's what I've learned about myself: I'm a talker and I'll ask you question after question to get to know you. Not everyone is like this, but I personally enjoy guys who are. I like not having to carry the conversation. I can carry the conversation, but I don't want to. I like a man that asks questions because it shows that he's trying to get to know me.

Preppy Texter tells me that he did the Paleo diet for Lent (explains the outdated pictures on Tinder), which sparks my interest because I too practice Lent. The waitress comes by and asks if we want refills. He waits silently for me to say something. I end up ordering us both a second round because he might not have. I'm okay with ordering my own drink, but feel that he should at least say something. I hate the uncertainty of this undefined "hangout" and wish he were more open and assertive.

While we talk, Preppy Texter starts checking his phone. At first, I think he's checking the time, so I don't mind it much. Then I notice him texting throughout our conversation. Apparently, he set up our "hangout" during the NFL Draft and is a huge Broncos fan (of course, a preppy sports guy). His friend is texting him to keep him updated in case the Broncos trade up. I'm trying to be a nonchalant cool girl, but am also thinking, "This is rude."

I'm unsure if this "hangout" can qualify as a date, but I'm nothing if not determined. Axelrad is adjoined to a pizzeria called Luigi's. I make mention about getting a slice of pizza because I need there to be food involved if I'm going to count this as a "date" (and, I'm hungry). It's pizza by the slice, so I'm optimistic. I order a $4 slice of vegetarian and he pays. We sit outside and wait until the pizza arrives.

Preppy Texter says he's ready to leave and meet up with his friend to watch the end of the draft. I get that we just met, but I'm getting mixed signals. I had set plans with him, and his friend did not. Before he ditches me, Preppy Texter tells me he is going out of town this weekend but will text me about getting together next week. We exchange a hug partnered with a side kiss on the cheek from his side. As soon as I pull away, he goes for it and plants one on my lips. We walk separately to our cars.

**Takeaways**: I'm confused. Was this a date? Compared to my standards, I would say NO. How did I end up kissing this guy if it wasn't a date? I would go on a second "date" with him, but his texting threw me off. He's into me enough to kiss me at the end of this "hangout", but not enough to have the common courtesy to put away his phone.

# DATE DIARY: TOO GOOD TO BE TRUE

April 30, 2016

**Date's Nickname**: Too Good to be True

**Age**: 24

**Occupation**: IT Business Analyst

**How We Met**: Bumble. After messaging every day for a week, I initiate a meet up.

**Where We Went**: Dinner–Tsukiji Sushi

**What I Ate**: Edamame and an avocado & cucumber roll

**Total Cost Estimate**: $14

**Prior Expectations**: I know this guy is different. He's sweet and messages me almost every day. Probably looking for a relationship, which I'm open to.

**Date Diary**: Before we decided on a dinner spot, I informed him of my vegetarianism. I can make do at almost any restaurant, therefore I'm not picky when it comes to dinner spots. Too Good to be True chooses a sushi bar. I arrive before him and wait at the hostess table.

**First Thoughts**: He's taller than me. Fit. Southern. Looks a little too much like my brother.

We sit across from each other at a booth, and he tells me I can order anything I want. I get edamame and an avocado and cucumber roll because I'm boring. We've been in constant communication for almost two weeks (I'm not normally a texter), and I end up forgetting some details of our conversation. Can you blame me? I'm messaging many boys every day. The more we talk, the more I like him.

Too Good to be True is the total package.
- Attractive. Is 6'5" and fit.
- Stable. Has a great job.
- Ambitious. Is currently studying for the GMAT.
- Kind Hearted. Is dog sitting his friend's dog while he's out of town, bought the dog toys, and stayed home from work to care for it.
- Social. Asks me lots of questions.
- Considerate. Clearly chose this sushi restaurant just for me judging by the way he handles chopsticks.

If I had to create a list of attributes that a man would need to have in order to marry me, he would exceed them all (okay, I may be getting ahead of myself). However, there's one small problem. The entire time at dinner, I cannot stop thinking about how much this guy looks like my brother. His facial features, his physical features, and even the way he speaks remind me of my brother. Intellectually, he's nothing like my brother, but he's so physically similar to my brother that it's distracting.

We end up spending two hours at the restaurant before deciding it's time to leave. I informed him prior to our date that I had a friend's birthday party to attend later that night. The bill comes, and he already has his card out. I offer to pay.

He laughs and says, "Yeah, right."

Before we leave, I head to the restroom. As I walk back in the direction of our table, I see him waiting for me at the front door. We walk out of the restaurant, exchange hugs, and head off in different directions.

**Takeaways**: I like this guy. I want to date him. I'm not sure if I can get over the looking-like-my-brother thing, but he's so great that I'm willing to try. The hard part about these dates is that I only know what I'm thinking. I have no clue what these guys think about me. Therefore, by the rules, I'll have to wait and see if he likes me enough to initiate a second date.

# DATE DIARY: BRUNCH ENTHUSIAST

May 1, 2016

**Date's Nickname**: Brunch Enthusiast

**Age**: 25

**Occupation**: Engineer

**How We Met**: Tinder. He writes on his profile "Brunch Enthusiast." I initiate a conversation about local brunch places and within six messages he asks me out to brunch.

**Where We Went**: Brunch–Liberty Kitchen Oyster Bar

**What I Ate**: Cheese omelet and a mimosa

**Total Cost Estimate**: $19

**Prior Expectations**: I'm not quite sure what this date will be like. He seems a little nerdy. Not sure how social this engineer will be.

**Date Diary**: I arrive before him and put our name on the wait list. He arrives shortly after and informs the hostess that he called ahead. I'm immediately impressed and know I will not be paying for this meal.

**First Thoughts**: His pictures are a little outdated. I don't remember a beard in any of the pictures. He looks much older in person. I'm thinking the beard could've heavily influenced this. He's a little too skinny for my taste.

Brunch Enthusiast orders us mimosas. The typical date conversation starts. I'm really getting good at answering the question "What do you do for fun?" I date online. Brunch Enthusiast starts telling me about his love for mimosas and day drinking. I learn very quickly he's into day drinking more than "brunch." His friends go to "brunch" every weekend at Cyclone Anaya's for the bottomless mimosas.

Here are my next thoughts:
- Thank you very much for the bottomless mimosas information. I'll probably run into you there next week when I'm on another brunch date.
- Do you even care about the brunch food? Or is it just mimosas? (I ask him if he was a waffle/pancake guy and he says NO). Point proven.
- You cannot qualify yourself as a brunch enthusiast in Houston when you go to Cyclone Anaya's every weekend but have never been to Liberty Kitchen or Benjy's.

Needless to say, he orders us another round of mimosas. Keep them coming Brunch Enthusiast! We start a conversation about his friend's start-up app. It has something to do with bars and social media (go figure). It's supposed to be a live video of the "Atmosphere" (it's the name of the app). Essentially, you would be able to see the events going on at a bar before you commit to going there. From my understanding, it's an app that tells you where the party is.

Brunch Enthusiast asks what I'm doing the rest of the day. I tell him about my plans to go to the art festival at Memorial Park, and he tells me he's going to a midtown bar to meet up with his app friends. I think he wanted to invite me but, since I already had plans, doesn't extend an invitation. He pays (this time I don't offer), I thank him, and we hug before heading in opposite directions.

**Takeaways**: I had a great time with Brunch Enthusiast, but I think we would be better as friends. I'm not sure I would go out with him again in a romantic setting. I've noticed that I'm starting to compare not only the dates, but also the guys. There are a few guys that I like and others I care less about. The dates are starting to become mundane. We talk personal history, partnered by casual jokes. He pays (even if I offer), we hug, we say something along the lines of "great meeting you, we should do this again some time", we leave, and I wait to see if he ever contacts me.

# DATE DIARY: PFG & SHORT SHORTS

May 1, 2016

**Date's Nickname**: PFG & Short Shorts

**Age**: 28

**Occupation**: Investment Banker

**How We Met**: Tinder. He asks me to do "something." We make plans for dinner and drinks before he cancels on me (this is the same man that cancelled on me before my date with The Transient). He is very persuasive and asks me to go to an art festival with him on Saturday. This is my second date of the day (it can be done, ladies).

**Where We Went**: Event–Buffalo Bayou Art Festival
What I Ate: Nothing. He pays for my entrance to the festival and a glass of wine.

**Total Cost Estimate**: $25

**Prior Expectations**: Since he cancelled on me, my expectations were low. He texts me before we meet up about his festival attire. He wants to inform me that he is wearing a PFG (fishing shirt) and short shorts–typical frat boy. I responded with "you do you."

**Date Diary**: I meet PFG & Short Shorts at his townhouse. He lives walking distance from the park and asks if I want to meet him at his place. I say yes because it's practical. I don't mind meeting a stranger for the first time at his place of residence.

**First Thoughts**: I'm picking up some mixed signals. A bright blue PFG, khaki short shorts, very colorful Toms slip-on shoes, and a silver cross hanging from his neck (not sure what look he's going for). Receding hair line but not unattractive.

I park in his driveway, and we walk upstairs. He gives me a short tour of the townhome, which he owns (or claims to), before we Uber to the festival (I thought he said it was walking distance). PFG & Short Shorts is personable, easy to talk to, and interested in art. This art festival is a big event for him. The festival comes to town twice a year, and PFG & Short Shorts does not miss it. Last year he bought a $400 canvas painting and a soap dish. I quickly learn PFG & Short Shorts is on a mission. The mission is most likely to impress me by buying expensive art and get me drunk by offering me wine every five minutes.

As we walk around scouting for a masterpiece, PFG & Short Shorts runs into his boss. He introduces me as "a girl I just met on Tinder". Okay, not really. I wish that would've happened. We exchange brief words with his boss before separating. Then, it happens again. We run into his upper level boss and repeat the exact encounter. PFG & Short Shorts is truly art festival royalty.

At the next booth, PFG & Short Shorts tells me about his taste in music. He's a big Grateful Dead fan and has a fair share of stories to prove it. By the end of our festivities, PFG & Short Shorts buys a canvas painting of arithmetic guitar strings and a plexiglass oil painting of a calavera woman. Bizarre combination.

On the way home, PFG & Short Shorts gets into a conversation with our Uber driver about the singer-songwriter Tracey Chapman. Why? I don't know. These things just happen. I could feel the "I-want-to-hook-up-with-you-vibe." I'm not into one night stands, and plan on making a break for it as soon as we arrive back to his house. I help PFG & Short Shorts carry his two new masterpieces inside. I set them down, and he puts on a Tracey Chapman song. I automatically know that he's going to try something; I just don't know what it is. Eventually, he straight up asks if he can kiss me. I appreciate the question, so I say yes. He turns that one kiss into a make-out session, and I realize it's time to go. I tell him I should head out, and he makes some side comment about how if I stayed we'd probably have sex. At least he's honest. I get in my car and leave with the intention of never seeing PFG & Short Shorts again.

**Takeaways**: I had a fun time with PFG & Short Shorts. Honestly, it's one of the best dates I've ever been on. He was 100% looking to have sex with a girl he just met but was respectable about it (only if it was mutual). Clearly, we want different things. My decision about going out with him again is an easy NO. I don't expect him to reach out either.

# DATE DIAGNOSIS: WEEK ONE

May 2, 2016

    I'm alive. I went on eight dates in seven days. I learned: It's easy to go on a date every night if you're open-minded. I've learned I need to be pickier on these apps.

    A date doesn't have to involve food, but it usually does. I originally assumed that drinks/coffee is not a date because it's doesn't involve food. What's funny is, the two dates I went on that didn't involve dinner/brunch, the guys ended up kissing me. It makes me think that those guys are looking to "hook up" rather than enter a relationship; all the guys who had dates with sit-down meals didn't try anything. I have decided to remove the rule about dates having to involve food to count. Men may have alterior motives when they choose late night bars over plated dinners, but I'm still counting them as dates. My experiment, my rules. This social experiment is already changing the way I define dating.

    Guys are not good at dating either. After my two dates on Saturday, I made plans to go out. I wanted to meet guys in person to see if I could initiate a date through personal interaction. My friends and I are out at Dean's, a downtown bar and lounge, when I notice a group of attractive men sitting together. I ask them if they are a bachelor party (my go-to conversation starter when I see a group of men out at bars). They decline and don't keep up the conversation. Five minutes later, I notice one of the men swiping on Tinder. I start watching him. His friend notices and taps him on the shoulder.

As soon as he turns around, I say "If you see me, swipe right."

Finally, that broke the ice and we start a conversation. This boy is cute, and we are flirting. He ends up leaving the bar to go with his friends and doesn't ask me for my number or anything. I am livid. I did all the work for him, and the only thing he had to do was ask for my number. It seems like guys are more likely to ask you out over text because it's safer to be rejected by someone you can't see than someone right in front of you. Maybe I'm speculating and generalizing all men, but I'm getting so many strangers asking me out through the phone and no strangers asking me out in person.

In most situations, I let the man lead. Most of the men, so far, have initiated the date, so I let them lead. If I ask someone to hangout, I come up with a plan. Therefore, I expect them to do the same. I'm learning how different men approach dating, but I'm also learning that I'm a little too focused on the date instead of the guy. I should do what I feel, but I feel myself holding back to let the date unfold. No big deal, I'm just gambling with my love life.

Dating App Update: If you're looking to meet up with people, Tinder is where it's at. Statistically more people use Tinder. I deleted Okay Cupid because it's too overwhelming. Bumble is not exciting, and nothing comes of that app. Coffee Meets Bagel is by far my favorite. Happn and The Grade stay on my phone, but I rarely open them.

# Week Two

# DATE DIARY: PERFECT DATER

May 3, 2016

**Date's Nickname**: Perfect Dater

**Age**: 28

**Occupation**: Engineer

**How We Met**: Coffee Meet Bagel. After seven messages, he asks if I wanted to "grab drinks and go dancing." Due to scheduling conflicts, we settled on brunch.

**Where We Went**: Brunch–Gloria's

**What I Ate**: Migas and a mimosa

**Total Cost Estimate**: $18

**Prior Expectations**: I was impressed that once we made plans to hangout in person, he didn't continue a conversation over text. I personally like this because I want to get to know someone through personal interaction, not messages.

**Date Diary**: Church ran late and I showed up to Gloria's 15 minutes after our planned meeting time. He was at the bar by himself with half a glass of mimosa in front of him.

**First Thoughts**: He's wearing a bright yellow polo shirt and some jeans. Lots of muscles, tall, but still approachable.

My first words "Sorry, I'm late. Church ran long."

He replies, "No worries, I came straight from church too."

Not that I'm conventional when it comes to dating, but I never thought religion would be the first topic of conversation on a first date. In this case, it allows both of us to be very transparent within minutes of meeting. We continue the conversation at the bar while our table is prepared. I order a mimosa, and he hands the bartender his card before I can say anything (my type of man). I later come to the conclusion that I'm on a date with the quintessential "Perfect Dater."

The hostess leads us to our table, and Perfect Dater graciously asks which side of the table I would like. I order the migas plate, and he chooses an egg plate. He's a healthy eater (still my type of man). We spend the next two hours in nonstop conversation. I learn so much about his family: what both of his parents do for a living, where they live, and their opinions on both religion and economics. By the end of the date, Perfect Dater and I have a clear idea of who we both are and what we both want. To be honest, Perfect Dater is not the type of guy I normally go after. I'm glad we waited to get to know each other in person or I might have showed up with preconceived notions.

The check comes, and he hands the waiter his card. I thank him, and we walk outside. Before leaving, I tell him how much I appreciate him setting plans, sticking to them, and not feeling the need to get to know me through text messages. He seems a little taken back but flattered. We hug and exchange words about meeting up again soon. However, I have a feeling that will never happen, not because I wouldn't like to go on a second date with him, but because we both know it wouldn't work out in the long term.

**Takeaways**: I believe Perfect Dater is the "Perfect Dater" because he seems to know who he is and what he wants. During the entire date, he never seemed nervous. I felt comfortable saying and doing anything. I believe guys who approach dating this way will end up spending less time and money on girls who don't align with what they are looking for. If you know what you want, it's easier to decide on whether or not you want to continue dating someone. By being upfront on the first date, you spend less time and money on a girl who isn't what you're looking for. If I want cookies and you invite me to go eat, my first question is "Does this restaurant have cookies?" If you don't know what you want, it takes longer to order your food. Don't be the person staring at the menu because they can't decide between the desserts.

# DATE DIARY: METRO MAN

May 4, 2016

**Date's Nickname**: Metro Man

**Age**: 25

**Occupation**: Field Engineer

**How We Met**: Tinder. He initiates the messaging. I initiate the "hangout."

**Where We Went**: Dinner–Lowbrow's, a causal patio bar and grill

**What I Ate**: Cauliflower, Broccoli and Kale
Total Cost Estimate: $12

**Prior Expectations**: I purposely initiate a meet up because he's very attractive and I enjoy messaging him. I think he really appreciates how forward I am because he drives into town on a Monday night. My expectations are high.

**Date Diary**: Traffic is bad en route to Lowbrow's from work. I arrive after him in my perfected work-to-date-outfit. He is sitting by himself at a table in the front deck of Lowbrow's.

**First Thoughts**: Tall, very tall. Attractive, very attractive. Dresses very "country" (i.e. polo shirt tucked in, belt, blue jeans, boots). He pulls it off.

Metro Man greets me with a hug before I sit down. The minute we start talking, I pick up on a very friendly and feminine vocal tone, and it catches me off guard. Truth be told, I'm not into it, but it doesn't make me write him off. Metro Man and I easily keep up a conversation. He's social and can relate to many of my interests. Here are few of the topics we talked about:

- Our mutual love for Taylor Swift
- His love for animals and interest in getting a cat
- My distaste for cats (unless they're Taylor Swifts cats)
- His love of cuddling
- His need to live alone because he's had bad experiences living with boys in the past

I end up ordering two veggie sides for dinner because Lowbrow has limited vegetarian options, and it is steak night (this is the second time that's happened). The atmosphere at Lowbrow is great for a casual first encounter. By the time we finish dinner, I'm ready to leave. I have every intention of paying for my dinner, mostly because I initiated the meet up. The check comes, I offer, and he declines. I know there won't be a second date. I had the easiest time talking to him, and he's a friendly guy, but I was not feeling it. I tell him that I'm going to head to the restroom before leaving. We say goodbye before I head to the ladies' room and (like always) say something along the lines of "we should do this again."

**Takeaways**: You cannot judge a book by its cover. I thought Metro Man was my type of guy because of his profile pictures. There should be chemistry in a romantic relationship, and, no matter how good-looking Metro Man is, I didn't feel any sparks. It would be interesting for me to find out what he thought of our date. I wonder if he felt sparks or if it felt like friends hanging out. This is why you have to meet people in person. If I met this guy anywhere besides an app, I would've never initiated a date.

# DATE DIARY: CHEAP ASS

May 5, 2016

**Date's Nickname**: Cheap Ass

**Age**: 27

**Occupation**: Chemical Engineer

**How We Met**: Coffee Meets Bagel. He messages me about going to Aka Sushi (I mention it in my profile), and we make dinner plans within three messages.

**Where We Went**: Dinner–Aka Sushi

**What I Ate**: Two avocado and cucumber rolls

**Total Cost Estimate**: –$10

**Prior Expectations**: He seems very eager to hang out. We don't message much before meeting.

**Date Diary**: This was another work to date dinner. Due to traffic, I show up 15 minutes late. By the time I arrive, he's already sitting at a table and drinking sake by himself.

**First Thoughts**: He doesn't stand up when I met him at the table, which means I have no idea how tall he actually is. From the sitting position, he doesn't look 6'3.

Cheap Ass is apparently a sushi snob. He has this thing with wasabi. After I suggested Aka Sushi, he asked me how hot the wasabi is. As soon as I sit down, I explain why I love Aka Sushi: the happy hour at Aka Sushi is incredible. I've never ordered anything off their regular menu because you can pay half price for great quality sushi. I order two $4.25 rolls (yes, this is important) because I'm hungry, and they're only $4.25. He orders a "fancier" roll with spicy mayo and tempura. When the roll arrives, he shoves all the wasabi on his one roll.

Cheap Ass is a nerd. He's social, can carry on a conversation, and has a sense of humor, but he's just not confident in himself. At the end of the meal, the waiter leaves the check on the table. Most of the guys I've dated take the check right away. Cheap Ass lets it sit there. We keep up conversation between silent awkward pauses. A good three minutes pass, and Cheap Ass has not grabbed the bill. I can feel the awkward tension.

I break the silence, grab my wallet, and say, "Did you want to split it?"

Cheap Ass replies, "Yeah, that'd be great."

I'm a grown independent woman, but, according to my rules, this does not count as a date. After I pay for my meal, I'm ready to leave. I tell Cheap Ass I have a small group I need to head to (not a lie). Cheap Ass and I walk out of the restaurant (he is actually 6'3), hug, and say our goodbyes.

Today 9:55 PM

> Let's see each other again. Are you freeish soonish? Hope your group didn't devolve into chaos.

Later that night Cheap Ass sends me this text. I split checks on a first date if a.) I initiate plans or b.) we are just friends. Other than that, if I offer to pay, I'm being polite. I've never been more confused after a "date." I assumed Cheap Ass wasn't into me.

**Takeaways**: I'm not upset about paying. It's more about the principle of paying. If an engineer cannot afford to spend an extra $10 on a girl he's interested in, then he's more than likely a.) not generous enough or b.) doesn't know what he's doing. I will not be going out with Cheap Ass again. I like men who work hard. Relationships take sacrifice and work.

Three days later, I come across Cheap Ass on Tinder. Cheap Ass super liked me, which means I already know he swiped right. I swipe left, obviously.

# DATE DIARY: FOUL MOUTH

May 6, 2016

**Date's Nickname**: Foul Mouth

**Age**: 24

**Occupation**: Navy Seal

**How We Met**: Tinder. I message him first, and he asks me to get a drink with him, which I turn into a pizza date.

**Where We Went**: Dinner–Bollo Woodfired Pizza

**What I Ate**: Two glasses of Malbec and a veggie pizza

**Total Cost Estimate**: $35

**Prior Expectations**: We seem to be very compatible over text message. Unfortunately, I've learned messages can be misleading.

**Date Diary**: I keep telling my friends that I'll stop getting into cars with strangers, but here we go again. I receive a text saying, "Your Uber has arrived." I walk outside of my house and am greeted by a man in a black Chevy Tahoe.

**First Thoughts**: Mustache. Pretentious frat boy. All the signs are there: Tahoe, khakis, tucked in button down shirt,

Cole Haan loafers, and plaid argyle socks. I don't normally go for this type of guy, but this one is HOT (even with the mustache).

During the first five minutes of our conversation, I learn he has a foul mouth. Every other sentence includes the word "fucking." I'm no prude, but I am a lady. Foul Mouth drives us to Bollo–a pizzeria and wine bar off West Alabama. We sit outside on the patio and both order a glass of Malbec.

By this point, I'm fed up with his obscenity, so I ask, "Do you normally use the word fucking in every sentence?"

He quickly realizes that I'm not a fan and apologizes. Foul Mouth claims it's the result of the Navy Seals, which is understandable and becomes much less foul-mouthed.

I end up ordering a personal veggie pizza (no sharing) and he orders a meat pizza. Excluding swearing, Foul Mouth and I have a lot in common. From what I can tell, Foul Mouth was brought up well. He orders us both a second glass before I have time to respond to the waiter. By the end of this date, I'm really feeling Foul Mouth. This is the first time during Operation: *No Pay May* I want this date to end with a make-out (the two glasses of wine may have influenced this). Foul Mouth and I end up talking (and drinking) until the restaurant closes.

The waiter hands Foul Mouth the bill and I say something along the lines of "Oh, are you paying?"

He replies "Yeah, I got it" without looking at the amount (I love him).

I pick up my pizza box, with a half of a pizza in it, and take it home. Foul Mouth provides me with dinner, next day's lunch, and a slight buzz.

We hop back in the Tahoe, and he drives me home. He parks in front of my house and makes plans to take me out again. Before I get out, I pause to see if he is going to try anything, but, he doesn't make a move. I thank him and exit the Tahoe.

**Takeaways**: I loved every logistical thing about this date. The man picks me up, let's me order whatever I want, doesn't look at the bill, makes plans to go out again, and doesn't expect anything from me at the end. Because of this, I'm more attracted to him than any other man I've been out with. This date is my comeback. I felt more myself on this date because I was less concerned about whether he would pay and more concerned about being myself.

# DATE DIARY: DERBY DUDE

May 7, 2016

**Date's Nickname**: Derby Dude

**Age**: 28

**Occupation**: Engineer (does anyone do anything else in this city?)

**How We Met**: The Grade. After messaging for a week, he invites me to be his date to a Kentucky Derby party.

**Where We Went**: Event–Kentucky Derby party

**What I Ate**: Unlimited mint juleps and a caprese salad

**Total Cost Estimate**: $65

**Prior Expectations**: I love that he asked me to an event instead of coffee, drinks, or dinner.

**Date Diary**: Derby Dude calls me about the details of the day. We plan to meet at his friend's condo for drinks before heading to the event. I meet him in the lobby of his friend's building.

**First Thoughts**: He is tall and has a sweet face. His face is covered by a full beard. Derby Dude is rocking a seersucker suit. We accidentally match our outfits' color schemes (cream and white). During the entire event people asked if we planned our outfits.

Derby Dude walks me upstairs to introduce me to his friends. I assumed we would be going to this event with a group of guys and girls. In hindsight, I should have been more concerned about my safety because my assumption was wrong. His "group of friends" is two 30-year-old men. I'm in a strange condo with not one, but three men I do not know. Oh wait, I almost forgot–we're all drinking. Mom, don't read this.

Forty-five minutes later, Derby Dude orders us an Uber. When the Uber arrives, I take the front seat. On our way to the party, I joke about how these three men are squeezed compactly into the back of a Honda Civic. Prior to the event, I researched the ticket price. Turns out Derby Dude dropped $65 on my ticket (highest cost estimate yet).

First of all, if you've never been to a Kentucky Derby party, it's something you MUST do. The attire alone is worth it... so many hats. I am extremely impressed by one in particular. I ask the owner if I can try it on. He is so flattered by the question that he ends up taking a full-on photo shoot of me in his hat. Local vendors each provide their own take on the classic mint julep and encourage guests to vote on their favorite. I like to follow rules, so I comply. I'm a social girl, especially when I'm drinking. I spot a group of three girls who look my age and strike up a conversation. The old men take a hint and make their way over to my new kick ass girl squad. I take full credit for creating what turns out to be a solid party crew. These three girls, the three old men, and I spend the next two hours eating, drinking, and gambling. The seven of us are having such a great time!

I'm really digging this date except there is one thing missing: I'm rarely speaking to Derby Dude. With the excess of entertainment and people, I'm finding it hard to ask him intimate questions. We're having fun together, but I leave not knowing much about him. He didn't seem to mind because I later find out he gave one of those girls his phone number. After the party, I catch a ride with my new kick ass girl squad. I'm not a huge fan of Derby Dude. Nice guy, but not for me.

**Takeaways**: I had a fantastic time! This party was the highlight of my week. However, if you're trying to get to know someone, this might not be the best first date. I think these events are better if you want to see how someone interacts socially. I could see something like this being a great second or third date. I doubt I'll ever see Derby Dude again. I think leaving a party with other people rather than the guy you came with is a sign that the date didn't go well.

# DATE DIARY: ADJUSTER

May 8, 2016

**Date's Nickname**: Adjuster

**Age**: 26

**Occupation**: Private Investigator

**How We Met**: Coffee Meets Bagel. I message this guy all day. I initiate plans to grab drinks because I need a last-minute date.

**Where We Went**: Dinner and Drinks–Axelrad and Luigi's Pizzeria (my go-to spot)

**What I Ate**: Veggie pizza and a cider

**Total Cost Estimate**: $8

**Prior Expectations**: His profile doesn't WOW me, but he consistently responds to my messages.

**Date Diary**: The only thing that stands out about this guy is that he keeps adjusting himself. Seriously, that's the only thing I noticed.

**First Thoughts**: He dresses very boyish. Striped polo shirt, Reeboks, and blue jeans. There is no initial attraction.

I arrive before him, order myself a cider, and strike up a conversation with the bartender. A few minutes later, Adjuster shows up and orders himself a beer. We find a bench outside under the neon-lit tree (an Axelrad staple). We exchange the typical back-and-forth questions. I purposely pause and to see what questions he will ask me. "Did you play sports in high school?" *Dear future dates–Everyone on this planet asks me that question because I'm tall. Please ask me better questions. Deeper questions. Ask me about my love for Taylor Swift, my dietary restrictions, or ANYTHING else.* Adjuster tells me he's a private investigator. I'm intrigued until I find out what his job really entails. From what I understand, Adjuster is paid to sit in a car for 6-10 hours a day to spy on people. Basically, boring boy has a super boring job.

I mention something about grabbing a slice of pizza (might as well feed myself if I'm not going to be entertained). While we are waiting in line for a slice at Luigi's, I begin to really notice his "adjusting." It happened so often that I start to worry. (Dude, you should probably schedule a doctor's appointment). By the time our pizza arrives, Adjuster is at the bar grabbing the next round of drinks.

As he makes his way back with my cider, I notice some more adjusting. We carry on a pleasant conversation, nothing too exciting. After my last sip of cider, I excuse myself to the ladies' room. I return and ask Adjuster if he's ready to head out. Before we leave, Adjuster asks for my number. I give it to him, partnered with a final goodbye hug.

Takeaways: Adjuster is a sweet person, and I had a good but not a great time. He probably has the qualities to make a good boyfriend, but I don't want good, I want great. I'm not sure if I would give him another shot. Should I go out with him again?

# DATE DIAGNOSIS: WEEK TWO

May 8, 2016

I wrapped up week two with six dates (five if I don't count the one where I paid for my dinner).

Here's a list of things I learned:

THIS IS EXHAUSTING. I'm physically and emotionally drained. I wake up and spend 9 hours at work. During work, I try to find time for the occasional right swipe and a witty response to a text. As soon as I leave work, I drive to a date or to my house to switch clothes for a date. I relive the same conversation every day and reassure myself that it's JUST ONE MONTH. I can do it. I must do it.

I'm interested in about one out of every seven guys I date, which means, I have to go on six "okay" dates in order to go on one great one. The odds are not in my favor. I've noticed that the men I'm interested in are the ones where I initiate either the messages or the date itself, but (for some reason) the men who are more proactive and easier to meet end up being men I don't care for. I'm unsure of how this experiment will end. Will I go on 31 first dates with 31 different men? At this point, I've had no second dates.

I set out on this social dating experiment to learn about dating. I want a chance to date guys I normally wouldn't. I've learned that I can't judge a book by its cover, and to hold off my assumptions based on someone's personality over text messages.

Dating App Update: I deleted Happn this week. I never opened it. The layout sucks, and I don't have time to scroll through hundreds of profiles and waste perfectly good iPhone storage space (we all know how precious that is). Coincidentally, one of my dates this week mentioned the dating app Hinge. From his perspective, Bumble is the new Tinder, and now Hinge is the new Bumble. I thought, why not give it a try?

News: My initial plan was to go on a date every night, consecutively. I've since revised this. One night this week, I needed a break. Not because I couldn't go out with someone, but I didn't want to. I needed time to myself; I've haven't hit the gym since this experiment began and noticed a little less definition in my arms. I went on eight dates last week, so I figure it evens out. New goal: 31 dates in 31 days. I don't have to go on a date every night. I can have two dates on one day and no dates on another day. The principle is still the same.

# Week Three

# DATE DIARY: HINT DROPPER

May 9, 2016

**Date's Nickname**: Hint Dropper

**Age**: 25

**Occupation**: Graduate student

**How We Met**: Tinder

**Where We Went**: Dinner and Drinks–Axelrad and Luigi's Pizzeria

**What I Ate**: Slice of veggie pizza and a cider

**Total Cost Estimate**: $15

**Prior Expectations**: Here is our first textual experience. I'm impressed by how forward he is. I dislike the idea of hanging out, and I don't really like "grabbing drinks," but I decide meeting this guy at 9:30 pm on a week night is worth it. I love when a man is straightforward.

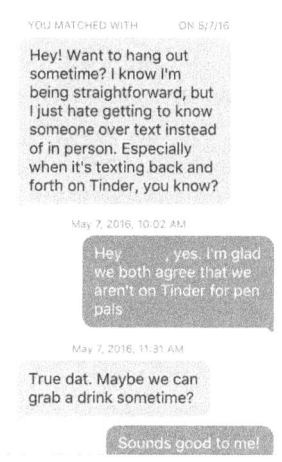

**Date Diary**: Hint Dropper arrives before me. He sends a text asking if I would like a slice of pizza. I respond with "Just one slice of vegetarian. No black olives. Thanks!" I love that he hasn't met me yet but is generous enough to spend $4. As I walk into Luigi's, Hint Dropper hands the cashier his card (perfect timing).

**First Thoughts**: Better looking in person than in pictures. Facial hair. (Can I get at least one clean shaven face?) He's wearing flip flops. This may sound pretentious, but I believe flip flops should only be worn for outdoor water activities. I'll let flip-flops slide when you're running a quick errand, but not on a date, especially when you're on a date with a true fashion queen.

I offer to pay for the first round of drinks. He orders a beer, and I stick with a cider. Axelrad is full tonight and there are only a few seat options. Unfortunately, we sit side by side at a picnic table with another couple facing the opposite direction. It's a bit easier to communicate when the person is directly in front of you. It feels like I'm doing neck exercises on this date.

Hint Dropper is very social, and I become more interested as we talk. Hint Dropper is the type of guy I would never pick out in a crowd, but he has potential.

Suddenly, the date goes from 100 to zero. As soon as we finish our first round, Hint Dropper is caressing my back, my legs, and my arms. He grabs my hand and looks straight into my eyes. I give a dog a bone and kiss him. He starts asking fewer questions about me and more questions about what we're doing later.

For example, Hint Dropper asks, "Is your roommate comfortable with you bringing guys back to your house?"

I just met you. I know he just wants to hook up, so I decide to play a game. I'm curious to see if Hint Dropper will ask me directly if we're going to have sex.

Hint Dropper: "Do you want to go to another bar?"
Me: "Why?"

Hint Dropper: "For another round."

Me: "We can get another round here; I don't see why we need to drive somewhere else. Plus, I have work tomorrow and don't need to be out too late."

Hint Dropper: "Well, this bar is more secluded. We can take my car there."

Me: "Seems like a waste of time to drive to another bar just for a drink."

Hint Dropper: "Okay, do you want to go somewhere more private?"

Me: "No. I'm okay here."

After that, Hint Dropper goes to the bar to get the next round. This seems so juvenile. We're adults. He should have the guts to say what he wants instead of dropping hints, even if I am going to say no. When he asked to hang out, I assumed he wanted to get to know me; if he was looking to hook up, he should've been honest about it. It would've saved us time, effort, and money.

By the time we leave the bar, he's still dropping hints. He offers to walk me to my car, which I reject. We hug and he goes in for another three kisses.

**Takeaways**: The saddest part about this whole thing is I was into him until he started dropping hints. I could see myself wanting to be with him, but my interest evaporates as soon as seduction became the goal. Here's what I think: Tinder does have a hook-up reputation, but it's wrong for a man to assume every girl on Tinder will sleep with him on the first date.

# DATE DIARY: FUTURE BOYFRIEND

May 10, 2016

**Date's Nickname**: Future Boyfriend

**Age**: 24

**Occupation**: IT Analyst

**How We Met**: Bumble. At 8:15 p.m., I sent him a message about grabbing drinks tonight, and we are both at the bar by 9:30.

**Where We Went**: Drinks–Porch Swing Pub

**What I Ate**: Two ciders (I'm not a beer girl. I'll probably gain a little weight from all the sugar I've had this month. Next month will be Run Every Day June.)

**Total Cost Estimate**: $14

**Prior Expectations**: I originally have dinner plans with a different guy for tonight. He cancels our dinner at 2 p.m., but then wants to meet up for drinks later in the evening. I'm game, so I agree to drinks instead of dinner. At 8:00 p.m. he cancels on our drink plans. Here is our text conversation on how I handled the situation.

> The fact that you can't set plans kinda pisses me off
>
> But nothing else really

You're quite forward. It makes it very easy to understand what you want from me.

Which I struggle with at times

> I'm just trying to figure out while you're on a dating app if you don't actually want to meet people
>
> Get it together

It seems like more work to keep up with a relationship over text than a relationship in real life. Plus, I can't make out with my phone. Boys are stupid. Fortunately, Future Boyfriend swoops in and agrees to meet me within minutes of setting plans. These are the men I like, the men I need.

**Date Diary**: I arrive to the bar first and ask him if he wants a beer. I initiated plans and have every intention of paying for not only my drink but also his.

**First Thoughts**: He is tall and attractive. He's wearing flip-flops.

We sit at a table in the back. I could care less whether he's paying, so I'm much more open. Throughout the course of hyper-dating, I've stopped wondering why my dates behave certain ways and have grown numb to boys cancelling on me. All I want to do is drink. I think Future Boyfriend can sense I'm tense and strikes up a conversation. We're essentially in the exact same stage of life. Both of us recently graduated college, are working in similar fields, and looking for new adventures. I start telling him about my recent trip to Spain. Turns out every young American tourist that visits Barcelona goes to the same clubs. Not only did Future Boyfriend and I share in the same Barcelona night life, but we also took the exact same cooking class, just 10 months apart! Our commonalities inspired another round. I told the bartender to put it on my tab!

By the end of the date, it's clear that Future Boyfriend and I are attracted to each other and have common interests, but what happens next makes my heart flutter. The bartender kept my credit card when I started my tab. When we decide to leave, Future Boyfriend goes to the bartender, exchanges our cards and pays for all our drinks. CHIVALRY IS NOT DEAD. We walk out of the bar, and he asks me for my number. I hope he asks me out again.

**Takeaways**: I want to date a guy who wants to date me. I want a guy who likes me enough to go out of his way to make plans and commits to them. I want a guy that will pay because he likes me enough to pay. Here's the thing, you just need to be confident in who you are and what you want. If you want to date me, impress me.

# DATE DIARY: BRUSSELS SPROUTS

May 12, 2016

**Date's Nickname**: Brussels Sprouts

**Age**: 24

**Occupation**: Engineer

**How We Met**: Bumble. He ask me to go to dinner or drinks with him anytime this week.

**Where We Went**: Dinner–Benjy's on Washington

**What I Ate**: Crispy brussels sprouts, quinoa and market vegetables

**Total Cost Estimate**: $30

**Prior Expectations**: I'm impressed by his choice of restaurants. My friends have been telling me about the brussels sprouts at Benjy's for months. From his profile, I can tell he's very tall!

**Date Diary**: Before my dinner date, I meet up with a girl friend for happy hour at Bovine & Barley. After a glass of wine, my friend and I tell the bartender about Operation: *No Pay May*. The bartender becomes interested in this topic. I ask him about his dating history and what he would classify as a date. He tells me that he would rather invite girls to events or shows instead of drinks or dinner. However, he isn't an active dater. At this point in his life, he's focusing on becoming a better person. I completely understand and agree with him. It's easier to know what you want when you know who you are. Good for him.

I Uber to Benjy's due to three glasses of Malbec. The good news? I'm already buzzed. Alcohol kills the nerves. I arrive before Brussels Sprouts and wait for him at the hostess table.

**First Thoughts**: He's very tall, the tallest guy I've dated in May, and cute.

The hostess sits us in the back corner booth (guess we aren't dressed well enough). He starts with beer, and I start with brussels sprouts. From this point on, I'm equally as into my brussels sprouts as I am my date.

Brussels Sprouts loosens up after a beer, and his go-with-the-flow attitude coaxes me to confide the struggles of my workday; dear coworkers, it's not you… it's me. Brussels Sprouts is great and a super social guy, even more so with the alcohol.

I'm enjoying Benjy's very much. I order the quinoa and market vegetables as my entrée.

Brussels Sprouts and I stay at the restaurant for two hours, joking and laughing. The waiter places the check on the table, and Brussels Sprouts reaches for it (Ba Da Ba Ba Bah, I'm Lovin' It!®). We exit the restaurant, hug, and he tells me he'll text me, which he does later that night.

**Takeaways**: First off, go to Benjy's and get the brussels sprouts. This is a date diary, not a food review, so I know what you're thinking: what about the guy? Food might be the way to a man's heart, but unfortunately the food found its way into my heart and the man did not. Besides his height and good looks, Brussels came across… plain. My friend has a theory that attractive, tall men have less personality because they don't have to work as hard to attract women, whereas short men must develop more personality to woo women. I am not saying I agree or disagree with this theory, but it seems to apply in this circumstance. Still no kiss after dinner. I would've been into it, just saying.

# DATE DIARY: SWEET INTENTIONS

May 13, 2016

**Date's Nickname**: Sweet Intentions

**Age**: 26

**Occupation**: Electrical Engineer

**How We Met**: Coffee Meets Bagel. He sends me three messages to which I never respond. He sent a final message asking me to dinner, which I accept.

**Where We Went**: Dinner–Izakaya, a Japanese-style tapas restaurant

**What I Ate**: Shishito peppers, edamame, mushroom mac and cheese, the Fuku Bounce cocktail

**Total Cost Estimate**: $50

**Prior Expectations**: I'm super impressed by his willingness to take out a girl he's never met before to a fancy dinner. To be honest, if he hadn't asked me to dinner, then he probably would've gotten lost between all the other boys.

**Date Diary**: He's sitting at the bar drinking whiskey by himself when I arrive (most likely to kill the nerves).

**First Thoughts**: He's tall, attractive and nerdy. Really nervous.

Immediately, I can tell that Sweet Intentions does not do a lot of dating. For the first 15 minutes, he has a hard time looking me in the eye. I can't tell if he's socially awkward with all people, all girls, or just with first dates. The hostess leads us to our table and explains the menu. I informed Sweet Intentions of my dietary restrictions prior to our date, so I'm not sure why he chose a restaurant intended to share dishes if he's a meat eater.

After talking to Sweet Intentions for an hour, I realize he is extremely intelligent and has big dreams, but seems to have a hard time fitting in. Sweet Intentions fills the awkward pauses with interesting questions and tangent stories. I'm impressed by how hard he's trying. Sweet Intentions lets me order a few veggie tapas along with his ceviche.

At the end of the night, he jokes that he thought I would stand him up. This saddens me, especially since he seems to lack the self-confidence to not take it personally.

I ask Sweet Intentions why he thought I might not show up and if anyone has ever done that to him.

He says, "No, no one has ever stood me up."

I respond by saying, "I would never do that to you, or anyone. That's not the type of person I am."

The bill comes and he lets it sit there. I know he's letting it sit because he wants to keep conversation going. Sweet Intentions called ahead and made a reservation; there is no way he isn't paying.

Sweet Intentions invites me to grab ice cream with him after, and I gently reject him because I made previous plans. I hug and thank him as we leave. I'm sure I'll talk to Sweet Intentions soon.

**Takeaways**: Long term, I know this relationship will most likely not work out. However, Sweet Intentions is one of the nicest guys I've had the pleasure of dating. I don't think it's fair for me to write him off after one date when he worked so hard. Yes, I will go out with him again. I prefer his sweet intentions over any hint droppers.

# DATE DIARY: BIRD POOP

May 14, 2016

**Date's Nickname**: Bird Poop

**Age**: 25

**Occupation**: Engineer at NASA

**How We Met**: Coffee Meets Bagel. He sends me his phone number and asks if we can hangout. (Boys, set a plan instead of an undefined hangout).

**Where we went**: Drinks–Onion Creek

**What I Ate**: Frozen Blue Moon and fried pickles

**Total Cost Estimate**: $20

**Prior Expectations**: We don't message much before meeting and set plans a week in advance.

**Date Diary**: My coworker asks if I can watch her Corgi this weekend while she is out of town. I agree and know this dog will be a hit with my dates. My date plans to meet me at my house. It's not the safest option, but I don't want to go to his house.

**First Thoughts**: He's good looking except for his teeth, which are crooked. Tall and dressed very casual. Drives a nice white Jeep.

From the start, I am not into this "date" compared to others because I am the one making all the plans, even though he asked to "hang out". I choose Onion Creek and bring along my borrowed Corgi. *Normally, I would never choose Onion Creek as a first date spot because it has a counter service, which makes the payment situation undefined and awkward. Then again, I am not sure if this is an actual date.

Bird Poop offers to buy me a Frozen Blue Moon while I wait with the dog outside. Several women stop by my table to play with the dog. Effortlessly (and unwittingly), I become a chick magnet. I have an epiphany about why so many men have pictures with dogs on their dating profiles. I completely get it now.

Bird Poop makes it back to the table with two Frozen Blue Moons and fried pickles to share. We talk about our jobs and family history. I quickly find out that he lives in Clear Lake. I don't know why a single 25-year-old man would live outside the loop. I'm sure the commute plays a role in his decision. THEN, IT HAPPENS.

While we're talking, a bird poops on his shoulder, like runny bird poop. It's hilarious! It takes a painful amount of restraint to not laugh at his expense. Bird Poop excuses himself to the restroom to wipe off his shirt. I wonder if it's wrong that I'm thinking, "I cannot wait to write about this later!"

Bird Poop makes it back to the table, and I try to say something comforting. We laugh it off and continue talking about my favorite subject: dating apps. We bond over our mutual distaste toward meeting people online, which, ironically enough, is how we met. Dating apps are more work than meeting people in real life. There are more options, more messages, more matches, more everything. What's wrong with going up to an attractive girl/boy you see in public and saying, "Hi, I would like to take you out sometime?" The worst thing they can say is no.

Bird Poop and I spend a couple of hours together before heading back to my house. Bird Poop drops me off and says the same thing all the other boys say, "We should do this again sometime."

**Takeaways**: I've always liked confident men, men who make a plan and carry out that plan. Truthfully, I'm not into Bird Poop and don't think we will ever hang out again, but he did provide me with great material for comic relief. Poor guy, I hope he wasn't too embarrassed.

# DATE DIARY: DONUT HOLE

May 15, 2016

**Date's Nickname**: Donut Hole

**Age**: 25

**Occupation**: Abercrombie and Fitch Manager

**How We Met**: Hinge (my first Hinge date!)

**Where We Went**: Brunch–Union Kitchen

**What I Ate**: Bottomless mimosas, Nutella donut holes and a potato, egg, and cheese breakfast taco

**Total Cost Estimate**: $20

**Prior Expectations**: Donut Hole initiates the messages and the meet-up. He sends a text that reads "U like mimosas?" Not very eloquent… but yes, who doesn't like mimosas?

**Date Diary**: I'm all about these brunch dates. Union Kitchen does bottomless mimosas on Sundays! It's possibly the cheapest way to get drunk. Needless to say, I left this brunch date a little tipsy.
    Donut Hole is sitting at a table on the side patio when I arrive.

**First Thoughts**: He's good looking, tan, and skinnier than I prefer. He's wearing a blue and white striped Abercrombie & Fitch T-shirt (thankfully, no flip-flops). Why are you wearing an A&F shirt at the age of 25?

Donut Hole calls the waitress over to order mimosas and donut holes. Only after he orders does he turn to me and say, "Are you hungry? I ate already so I was just going get us donut holes."

The audacity. I'm upset thinking:

We are having brunch at 11:00 am on a Sunday. Did you eat before our date so you wouldn't have to pay for your breakfast and mine?

Of course, I'm hungry. I'm at a restaurant that serves bottomless mimosas. I WANT FOOD. Do you expect me to drink and not eat?

Dude, be polite and ask me next time before you assume I want donut holes. I'm more of an egg-and-vegetable kind of girl.

I end up ordering a breakfast taco because, yes, I am hungry. If this donut hole doesn't want to pay for it, then he shouldn't, but I'm ordering some food. If you ask me out and intend to pay, let me order what I want. I will pay for it if you think what I order is "too expensive."

Once I receive my breakfast taco, I'm much less hostile. Donut Hole explains that he's in the middle of a career change. He recently quit his job in sales and is planning on teaching high school in the fall. Donut Hole is very sweet and social. He tells me I'm his first Hinge date, and I tell him he's mine (he is my first HINGE date, but far from my first online date). We start a conversation about online dating. Donut Hole tells me that girls tend to go silent in the text conversation as soon as he initiates plans. My ground-breaking hypothesis? Girls find meeting up with randos from the internet sketchy. Before this month, I would never let a stranger pick me up at my house, and I'm still not 100% certain I like meeting men online. However, this month is all about learning. Women, say "yes" sometimes. If anything, you'll have a story to tell. Trust me; I have plenty. Our conversation dies off.

The waitress brings the bill, and I offer to pay.

Donut Hole says "No, my mom says chivalry is not dead. I got it." Mothers know best.

We walk off the patio and pause to talk before heading to our cars. Donut Hole tells me he's going out of town next weekend but would like to get brunch again sometime. He sends me a text later that day, but it's not about making plans.

**Takeaways**: Here's what I think: if boys want to take initiative, they will. If they want to ask a girl out, they will on their time. I would go on a date with Donut Hole again, but I can't promise I'll still be interested in two weeks. Maybe men should realize women have timelines too, and if they don't take initiative, there are 31 other guys out there who will.

# DATE DIARY: FOUL MOUTH PART TWO

May 15, 2016

**Date's Nickname**: Foul Mouth

**Age**: 24

**Occupation**: Navy Seal

**How We Met**: Tinder. This is our second "date" (see Foul Mouth–Part One).

**Where We Went**: My house

**What I Ate**: Nothing

**Total Cost Estimate**: $0

**Prior Expectations**: Foul Mouth wants to "hangout". I invite him over to my house to play with my borrowed dog. He brings his dog too.

**Date Diary**: First off, I cannot count this as a date.

Foul Mouth shows up in sweat pants and flip-flops. We sit outside on my patio, talking and playing with dogs. I hadn't seen him in over a week. We made tentative plans a couple times, and he backed out. Normally, I would be over Foul Mouth, but our first date was so good!

Nothing is defined about this "hangout". I'm

attracted to him and would like to make out, but I don't know what we are. Both of us are struggling to find topics to talk about. I'm trying not to spill my future radio plans (more information to follow), and he's trying to figure out how I feel about him. I begin to realize we're repeating a few of our first date conversations… or am I mixing him up with another date? Hey, it happens, especially with my quantity of dates. A week might not seem like a long time to him, but for me, it feels like forever.

During this time, my coworker and her fiancé stop by to pick up their dog. I tell Foul Mouth that I'm going to introduce him as "a boy I met on Tinder." He gets embarrassed and begs me not to say that (in actuality, I already told my coworker). I'm not sure why he's worried. If we start dating, I'm telling everyone that Foul Mouth and I met on Tinder. I'm not embarrassed!

After a few hours, Foul Mouth heads home with his dog, and I'm left wondering how to evaluate our status. We didn't go anywhere. We didn't eat or drink anything. We didn't kiss. We didn't hug goodbye. We just talked.

**Takeaways**: He said he wanted to hang out again soon, to which I responded with a "maybe." That took him by surprise. Like, what do you want Foul Mouth? Do you want to date me? Do you want to be friends? Do you want to hook up? It felt like two friends hanging out.

*My coworker told me it seemed like Foul Mouth and I had been dating for months. I didn't take this as a compliment. It was our second date–far too early for comfortable sluggishness. If you want to date me, then date me–is that asking too much?

# DATE DIAGNOSIS: WEEK THREE

May 16, 2016

I ended Week Three with seven dates… kind of. It's very clear to me that my definition and views on dating are my own, but the world isn't black and white.

I learned: I'm tired all the time. Between my job, dating, and keeping up with my online personality, I'm finding it difficult to keep up with my Date Diaries.

Why don't these guys initiate a second date? Women seem to be socialized into thinking that if a guy likes you, he will go out of his way to let you know, hence the movie "He's Just Not That Into You." Very few of these guys have initiated second dates. Is it me? Do I need to text them all the time for them to think I'm still interested? Do I scare boys? Why don't the good ones make a move? Maybe I'll just do all the work: ask them out, pay, make a move. I'm going to try it just to see what happ… no, never mind. That's not what I want.

Despite my best efforts not to generalize all men, it seems like men either want to hook up and not commit or get serious about dating when THEY are ready for it. I respect this, but don't believe all dating has to start seriously. You date to get to know someone. If meeting strangers over the internet makes you uncomfortable, you shouldn't be using dating apps.

My friends refer to Operation: No Pay May as a poor girl's Bachelorette. To me, it seems more like the movie 50 First Dates. Honestly, I was hoping for more second and third dates.

Dating App Update: I deleted The Grade. Not enough people use it. Like I've said before, I need the iPhone storage space. I've decided to experiment less with Tinder, and more with Hinge and Bumble. There is a social stigma to Tinder. It's sad but true. I don't want boys to pay for my dinner in hopes I'll sleep with them, because I won't. However, it's more work for me on both Bumble and Hinge. For boys to initiate plans, I must message them for a long time. I easily match with 20 men a day, and half of them initiate a message. I don't have time to message everyone. My advice? Men, initiate some plans.

# Week Four

# DATE DIARY: SUIT & TIE

May 17, 2016

**Date's Nickname**: Suit & Tie

**Age**: 27

**Occupation**: CEO and Founder of a startup

**How We Met**: Tinder. He super likes me but never messages. I initiate a message because his profile is witty and he's 6'4.

**Where We Went**: Dinner–Oporto Fooding House
    Second Stop–Front Porch Pub
    Third Stop–SHOT BAR (don't judge)

**What I Ate**: Charred vegetables, bread pudding, wine, and lots of liquor

**Total Cost Estimate**: $50

**Prior Expectations**: After messaging, I find out Suit & Tie lives in Austin, but is "headed to Houston next week." I'm digging our Tinder conversation, so I ask if he wants to meet up while he's here, though normally I don't date out-of-towners. Suit & Tie tentatively invites me to a fancy dinner with a group of potential investors. The catch: if I go to the dinner, both of us must pretend we're old friends from college. Apparently, it's unprofessional to tell people you met on Tinder. This is a first date story I can NOT pass up.

**Date Diary**: Suit & Tie does not confirm plans until 5 p.m. for a 6 p.m. dinner. I hate unset schedules, but I really want to go on this date. Thankfully, the risk is worth it. I arrive at Oporto, and Suit & Tie meets me out front.

**First Thoughts**: He's wearing a suit. I love men in suits. Damn, he's wearing glasses. I love men in glasses. The combination is FIRE. Am I right, ladies?

Suit & Tie introduces himself before we walk into Oporto. I find myself sitting at the end of a table with nine other men. Yes, that's correct, I'm on a date with nine men. Suit & Tie sits across from me and explains why I'm sitting at a table with nine men. Suit & Tie is the CEO of a small startup. His colleagues (high school friends) are in town pitching their product to a group of investors. Three of these men are the investors, and the other five are the colleagues. Suit & Tie wasn't lying when he told me this would be a FANCY dinner. The investors order dish after dish to share with the table: stuffed dates, shrimp, oysters, squid, paella– which contain all meat–brussels sprouts, bread (finally, food I can eat).

I explain why I'm not eating, and the investor on my right (who's paying for this meal) tells me to order something vegetarian. A beautifully plated dish of charred vegetables arrives. Suit & Tie insists I take a picture with my vegetable art, which I immediately ask for him to text to me.

So much is happening on this date. I'm a rather social girl, so having dinner with nine men is a cake walk. The hardest part is remembering to pretend like Suit & Tie and I already know each other. Both of us are asking what I like to call the typical "get-to-know-you questions." like where you're from, where you went to school, etc. If anyone is listening, they can tell we just met.

Two glasses of wine down, and I'm feeling great.

It's dessert time! Gelato, bread pudding, and tiramisu made their way to the table. I wish my everyday life consisted of nine men and unlimited food. What a story that would be!

After we're done with dinner, I thank the investors because they paid for my meal. The investors head out, and Suit & Tie invites me to Front Porch Pub for drinks with the colleagues. I'm having fun, and Suit & Tie is still in his suit, so I agree to drinks. In reality, this "date" is a GROUP date. Maybe my life really is the poor girl's Bachelorette.

The six of us choose a table on the front patio of Front Porch Pub. By now, all the colleagues know Suit & Tie and I met on Tinder. It wasn't hard to figure out. My facial expressions are too uncontrollable to make me a good liar (my eventual downfall), and I'm almost 100% certain Suit & Tie told them before dinner. Suit & Tie orders everyone the first round. I'm chatting with my dates about their business and the day's meeting pitch before Suit & Tie starts asking me about Tinder. Please take a moment to pause because I don't think you are ready for this.

I break my own rule and tell Suit & Tie about Operation: *No Pay May*. Here's how it happened.

He asked, "How many Tinder dates have you been on?"

My traitor of a face can't control itself.

"A lot?"

Insert facial expression.

"Any recently?"

Insert facial expression.

One of my rules is not to lie, and I'm curious what will happen, so I tell him everything about my pending mission.

His initial response is, "So you're just using me. I'm just a number…" … followed by immediate jealously.

Suit & Tie separates me from his friends to have a more "one-on-one" date experience. He starts asking me how this date compares to the other ones (all guys love competition). I'm strangely relieved; the truth set me free, so to speak. We talk about No Pay May for a while but move on to other topics. I tell him about my future career goals, and he offers his best advice as a CEO. It really did turn into much more of a "date" after I told him. A good hour passes before we rejoin the group. Suit & Tie and the colleagues want to keep drinking. I am reluctant because I had work and a radio interview in the morning, but Suit & Tie is still in the suit so... I take them to Shot Bar.

Shot Bar is the only crowded bar on a Tuesday night. Lots of men and young girls. I buy everyone the first round. I do– after all–have a salaried job. Suit & Tie is getting handsy, but I'm into it. By the end of the night, it's safe to say Suit & Tie and I were feeling each other.

**Takeaways**: The next day I receive these texts from Suit & Tie:

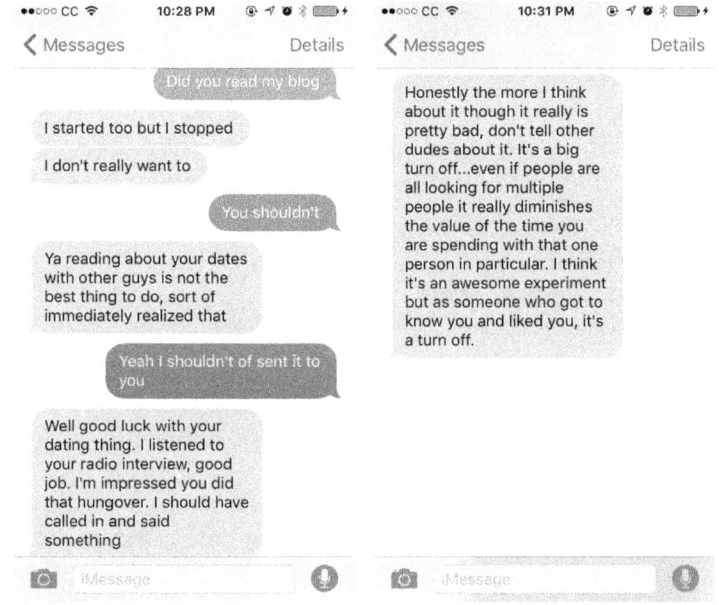

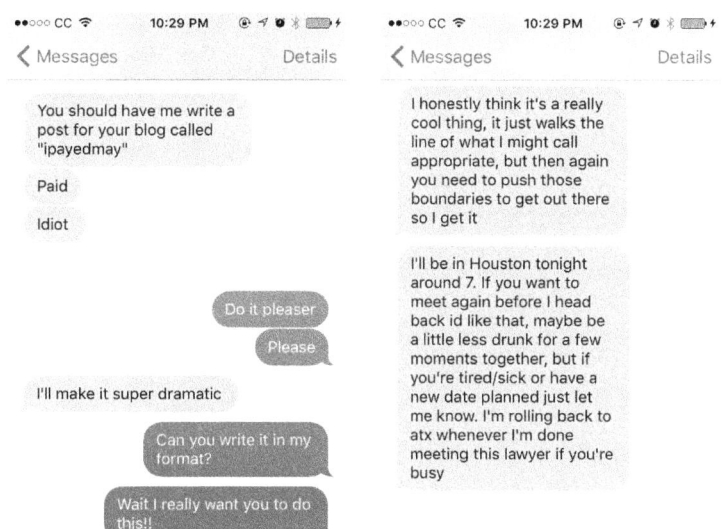

**Here's what I learned**: dating this many people in a short amount of time is not realistic, and makes men feel like a number. I regret telling Suit & Tie about Operation: *No Pay May* because it hurt his feelings, and I don't like hurting people—especially men I'm interested in. At the end of this month, I may end up alone (and I'm okay with that). But if a man told me he was dating 21 other girls on our first date, there would NOT be a second. If you're dating multiple people, you shouldn't talk about it on the first date. It takes away from the time you should be spending getting to know your date.

    It's almost impossible to date this many people and focus on one relationship. The idea that the more people you date, the more fulfilled you are is false. This idea of quantity over quality is a lie.

    Then again, this is the Catch 22: if I never told Suit & Tie about *No Pay May*, I'm not sure he would have asked me out on a second date.

# DATE DIARY: BIG PERSONALITY

May 18, 2016

**Date's Nickname**: Big Personality

**Age**: 29

**Occupation**: Financial Advisor

**How We Met**: Tinder. I send him a message that said, "We should date." Guess what… it works.

**Where We Went**: Dinner–Urban Eats, an upscale market and bistro

**What I Ate**: Skillet seared cauliflower and a glass of Malbec (it's Wine Wednesday!)

**Total Cost Estimate**: $20

**Prior Expectations**: His Tinder profile says, "Please have a big personality." I have a big personality. Men, be careful what you ask for!

**Date Diary**: We make plans to grab drinks this week. The day of our date, I text to confirm. He hasn't specified a location and asks me where we should go instead. I'm tired of choosing Axelrad and want real food. Urban Eats it is!

**First Thoughts**: He is tall and good looking. Dressed casual. He's wearing a black tank top under his gray cotton V-neck T-shirt. Interesting fashion choice.

Big Personality greets me with a hug and seems a little nervous. I initiate all conversation for the first ten minutes. I ask him a question. He answers. He doesn't return the question. So, I answer the question I asked him.

I order a glass of wine, and he orders the same. I'm obviously the initiator of everything on this date. Big Personality does not live up to his namesake. Maybe that's why he wants a girl with a big personality. He's not unsocial, just more generic. We manage to uncover a few common interests.

By the time dinner is served, Big Personality has more to say. He orders the sliders (an Urban Eats favorite), and I stick with vegetables. During our conversation, a thought stirs in the back of my mind: I think Big Personality is second-guessing everything he says. It's like he's scared to make a wrong move and needs to ask for my approval.

First dates are awkward, but there is no need to be a pushover. The best advice is… (pardon the corny cliché) –be yourself. Personally, I want someone to like me for me, not some temporary, pliable façade. I'm not going to order beer or meat and change who I am to impress people.

Big Personality and I are mid-conversation when the waiter drops off the check. It sits for a while before he grabs it.

I look at him and say, "You don't need to pay. I can pay for my meal."

With some hesitation, Big Personality says, "No. Don't worry about it. I'll get it." We wrap up our conversation and head outside.

Another awkward encounter: we exchange a hug, and Big Personality says, "Thanks for having dinner with me."

I respond with "No. Thank you for dinner. I had a great time." He's the one who bought me dinner, so I feel like I should be the one thanking him. I parked on the street, and Big Personality valeted.

As I'm walking away from him he says, "And if you didn't enjoy the company, at least you got free food."

I'm a little taken aback and respond, "What? I offered to pay." By this time, I'm a good 15 feet away from him and all dialogue ends.

**Takeaways**: As soon I get home, Big Personality sends me these texts. Not only is he over-analyzing himself, but he's over-analyzing me. Why can't two people just to go to dinner? If it doesn't work out, then it doesn't work out. No harm, no foul. I did have a great time with him, but I don't think he felt comfortable enough to be himself. It seems like he over thought our entire date. Dude, it's one date. CHILL.

# DATE DIARY: BANANA REPUBLIC

May 20, 2016

**Date's Nickname**: Banana Republic

**Age**: 26

**Occupation**: Engineer

**How We Met**: Tinder and Bumble. We start messaging on Tinder before the conversation fades out. We match again on Bumble. This time I send him my phone number (sometimes boys need a hint).

**Where We Went**: Drinks–La Grange, a patio bar

**What I ate**: Two classic margaritas on the rocks

**Total Cost Estimate**: $15

**Prior Expectations**: I originally had another date set up for this night, but he cancels (stupid boys). So, I pull out my little black book iPhone and ask a guy to meet me for drinks. Within an hour, I am on a date. If anything, *No Pay May* has taught me how easy it is to get a boy to meet up with me. I'm not sure if that's sad or impressive.

**Date Diary**: Before my date, I was at Pistolero's with a girlfriend for happy hour. Intrigued by my current dating mission, my friend agrees to observe my date from afar.

As I arrive at La Grange, Banana Republic messages me, asking what I like to drink. I ignore it because I'm 25 feet from the bar. He's standing by himself looking over the menu.

**First Thoughts**: He's tall and attractive. Dresses well. Looks older in person. For some reason, his photos on Bumble make him look boyish. He went in for a hand shake, and I went in for a hug. The hug wins. I ask for a classic margarita, and he pays.

We sit down at a romantic candle lit table for two. Banana Republic starts a conversation about his fancy watch. The conversation turns into a talk about where he shops–you guessed it–Banana Republic. I am a huge fan of Banana Republic and dressing in monochromatics. We make an instant connection. I work in the fashion industry and am very passionate about design, so I enjoy a man who cultivates a sense of style and stays on top of trends. After all, women don't need to be the only ones dressing for success. Please men, stop wearing flip-flops.

Banana Republic is very mature, the type of guy who's done everything right. Banana Republic is the quintessential modern-day gentleman. Every girl is looking for this type of guy: a chivalrous man with an attractive face and a stable job. After 30 minutes, I assume he's the I'm-looking-for-a-wife type. The aura of commitment overwhelms me. Don't get me wrong; I want to get married, but not at age 24.

To oversimplify, I find that men on dates are either looking for a wife or looking to get laid. Why can't men date a girl they like without the initial pressure of sex? Why do men only want to date when they're "ready" for marriage? I believe you can find someone you like, date them, and see if it works out.

Banana Republic stands up and orders a second round. One thing he says catches me off guard. Out of nowhere, he asks if I am a painter. Apparently, I have something white stuck to my arm resembling paint. I look down and see Wite-Out stuck to my elbow (work problems). After I respond with a negative, he tells me he thought that question was going to spark an interesting conversation about how I am a painter. I suppose even the most put together people have their awkward moments.

      Shortly after, Banana Republic and I exit La Grange. We hug and exchange a few words about how much fun we had. However, there is no mention of a second date.

**Takeaways**: Banana Republic did text me the next day. I'm not sure if he'll initiate a second date, especially since I initiated the first. I'm a busy girl these days, so if you want to see me again, send a few texts. Better yet, come up with a plan!

# DATE DIARY: ANAL BANDIT

May 21, 2016

**Date's Nickname**: Anal Bandit

**Age**: 28

**Occupation**: Biochemist

**How We Met**: Bumble. He initiates plans to "grab coffee" after a few days of messaging.

**Where We Went**: Coffee–Inversion Coffee

**What I Ate**: Two Americanos with soy

**Total Cost Estimate**: $10

**Prior Expectations**: I'm not into coffee dates… or Android users. How are we supposed to group message if your text messages are green? Strike one and two. My expectations are low.

**Date Diary**: Before you begin to worry about my safety, given my date's nickname, his nickname comes from a bizarre story he told me during our coffee date. His story involves one of his friends who was anally raped when they were in college. Although he and his friend reported the incident to the police, the officials were not able to disprove consent and did nothing. His friends made t-shirts that read "Anal Bandit" and wore them at the scene of the crime to prevent further altercations. While I understand the importance of addressing serious issues like rape, I could not wrap my mind around the fact that he was telling me this on our first date. For the remainder of the date, and well after, all I could think about was this traumatic story. Strike three.

Anal Bandit is sitting outside on the front patio waiting for me to arrive. We hug before walking inside.

**First Thoughts**: He's tall, fit, and put-together. Digging his style. I hate coffee dates; I'm hungry, but, as we walk up to the counter, I order only an Americano because Anal Bandit invited me out for coffee, not breakfast. If this situation arises in the future, I vow to order a breakfast taco, even if it breaks the rules of coffee dates. Anal Bandit pays for our coffee.

Anal Bandit initiates a conversation about dating apps (here we go again). Anal Bandit shares a few stories about his experiences meeting up with women through dating apps. Anal Bandit has bad luck with the women of the internet (except me, the experimental dater, of course). His first mistake is meeting girls from Okay Cupid. After he shares these stories, I understand why he meets women for coffee.

Anal Bandit asks if I want a second coffee. See, if he committed to something more than a coffee date, he could spend more time with me. I'm hesitant but agree to stay for another coffee. When Anal Bandit returns with our second coffees, I ask why he invites women out for coffee. Long story short, it's cheap and quick.

I take offense to this. When did it become okay to treat a woman's time and emotions like a drive-through? In and out in ten, with as little harm to the wallet as possible—but women aren't exactly putting their foot down. We women seem to be more willing to meet up with men off the internet for drinks or coffee rather than a sit-down meal. We meet up with them late at night following a "U up?" text message. I say this not to judge or blame women, but we've made it so easy for men these days. We've set our standards so low that men seem to have grown lazy.

Anal Bandit and I stay at Inversion Coffee for over an hour. He asks what my plans are for the rest of the day.

He says, "I don't have anything planned if you want to do something later."

I respond with, "Sure, let me know. I'm flexible with my schedule." I get the feeling that I'll have to text him if I want to "do something", but it's against my rules to initiate a second date.

**Takeaways**: Why? Why? Why? Anal Bandit is a great guy, truly. I would like to go on another date. But why is it up to me? Did you not initiate the coffee date and pay for my coffee?

# DATE DIARY: KISS CAM

May 24, 2016

**Date's Nickname**: Kiss Cam

**Age**: 21 (I accidentally broke a rule)

**Occupation**: College student (I swear I didn't know)

**How We Met**: Twitter. Yup, you read that correctly.

**Where We Went**: Astros' Game!
Second Stop–Lucky's Pub

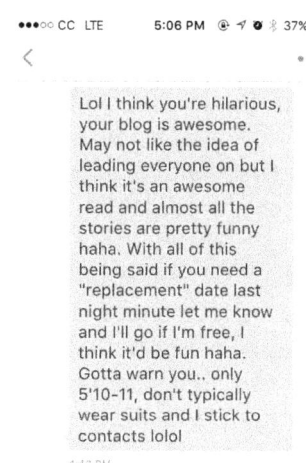

**What I Ate**: Peanuts, a Margherita pizza and a cider

**Total Cost Estimate**: $35

**Prior Expectations**: Since promoting No Pay May via social media, I've gained new followers. Kiss Cam sends me this message via Twitter direct message. Since Kiss Cam already knows about No Pay May, I'm not leading him on.

**Date Diary**: Kiss Cam makes plans for a double date to the Astros' game. Right away, I commit. This already sounds more fun than grabbing drinks. Kiss Cam offers to pick me up from my house before heading to the stadium.

**First Thoughts**: He's good looking and fit. Shorter then me (which I already know). Wearing a bright orange shirt and cutoff jorts (classic baseball game attire).

The first thing Kiss Cam says is "Wow, you're pretty." I suddenly realize Kiss Cam has not seen a picture of my face. Kiss Cam asked out Extra Cash Cathy, not me. Kiss Cam opens my car door before sitting in the driver's seat. On our way to the game, I realize I know nothing about Kiss Cam. It turns out he's a 21-year-old college student, and I have a minor freak out when I realize he's the same age as my younger brother. There is no way he is mature enough to viably date. Or maybe he is… boys have proved me wrong before.

Kiss Cam leads me to our seats and introduces me to the couple sitting beside us (we'll call them Jim and Pam). Jim works for the Astros and invites Kiss Cam to bring dates to the games. Kiss Cam and I bond over sports, family history, and more sports (we are at a sporting event). I learn that Jim and Pam know EVERYONE at this game. Jim and Pam are the Astros version of Barack and Michelle. Somehow, we all start talking about the kiss cam. Jim has the connection, he often threatens Kiss Cam with public embarrassment. Silently, I'm thinking these threats are about to become my reality.

The time comes. The video screen announces the "Kiss Cam." First Couple… not us. Second Couple… THAT'S US. I turn to Kiss Cam and give him a peck on the lips. I have to kiss on the kiss cam. Yup, our first kiss was broadcast in front of the entire stadium. Kiss Cam gets a flood of text messages from friends. Who knew Kiss Cam was so popular? Kiss Cam replied to a few "Was that y'all's first kiss?" text messages.

The shock of what just happened sets in. Kiss Cam seems a little embarrassed. However, I'm basically on Cloud Nine.

Who cares if everyone saw us kiss on camera? For me, a first kiss on camera is a once in a lifetime opportunity! Apparently, Jim can make that happen on a regular basis. After the dust settles, I decide we need a break from our seats. Kiss Cam and I leave to find the 50/50 jackpot tickets. As we leave our seats, I run into my college friend who lives in North Dakota. Could this night get any more random? Unfortunately, we make it to the jackpot ticket booth just as they announce the winner. Based on my odds that night, I bet if I would have purchased a ticket, I'd be $2,500 richer.

The Astros are tied at the bottom of the 10th. Kiss Cam and I decide that feeding ourselves is more important than the game's outcome (the Astros did end up winning at the bottom of the 13th–GO 'STROS GO!). Kiss Cam drives us to Lucky's Pub. I order a Margherita pizza and a cider. I want to pay for my own meal because he paid for everything else, but Kiss Cam won't let me (bless this boy!). We find a table right in front of a giant screen showing… the Astros' game.  Now that Kiss Cam and I have time alone, we talk about dating.

Kiss Cam and I talk about our views. I'm impressed by how much he wants to learn! The fact that Kiss Cam wants to know how women view dating shows me that he CARES. At the age of 21, he's already impressed me more than men 10 years his senior. Kiss Cam is a catch. College girls, get your fishing lines ready.

After dinner, we head back to the car. Kiss Cam opens my car door (I think I'll always love it) and drives me home. Kiss Cam parks and walks me to my door. I thank him, we hug, and he goes in for a second kiss. I think it's super cute and am flattered by the non-kiss-cam kiss.

**Takeaways**: This is exactly what a date should be. Two people having a great time, getting to know each other. Simple. No games (expect for baseball). No second-guessing. Just two people sharing an experience. Isn't that worth it? No matter if Kiss Cam and I spend one night together or the rest of time together, this date is something we share.

# DATE DIARY: SUIT & TIE PART TWO

May 25, 2016

**Date's Nickname**: Suit & Tie

**Age**: 27

**Occupation**: CEO of a startup

**How We Met**: Tinder. Second date.

**Where We Went**: Drinks–Bovine & Barley
Second Stop–Shay McElroy's Irish Pub

**What I Ate**: Two glasses of Malbec, tater tots, and later two vodka cranberries

**Total Cost Estimate**: $45

**Prior Expectations**: Suit & Tie is back in Houston on business. He makes plans to take me out on Thursday night, but (if he has time) wants to meet Wednesday night after a networking dinner. I tell Suit & Tie that I will leave my schedule open. I don't necessarily love unset plans, but I like Suit & Tie enough to sacrifice.

**Date Diary**: Suit & Tie finishes with his networking dinner at 8 p.m. We make plans to meet downtown at Bovine & Barley. I bump into the bartender from my Brussels Sprouts date. He's excited to see who my date is tonight (he ends up sending me an email the next day with rave reviews and discussion topics–see, *No Pay May* sparks discussion, it's not just a mission for free food).

Suit & Tie shows up in a new suit. I do have this thing about suits. I placed a wine order with the bartender before Suit & Tie arrived. Suit & Tie orders a beer and jumps into a conversation bragging about the dinners and experiences he had with the most well-known and wealthiest people in the country. His monologue, though interesting (I'd brag about something like that too), comes across pompous and narcissistic.

Suit & Tie orders another round and some tater tots. This 100% feels more like a date than the last time I saw him. Honestly, why would anyone invite a girl they've never met to a first date that involves dinner with investors. If Suit & Tie and I end up dating, our "how did you meet" story would be unreal.

After a couple of Malbecs, Suit & Tie wants a change in environment. As we walk to Shay McElroy's, Suit & Tie stops me for a quick kiss. We are holding hands and are very flirty. He orders me a vodka cranberry, and I make a mental note that I need to stop drinking on week nights. We head out to the patio and sit at a table.

Suit & Tie offers me career advice. Both of us are extremely driven, hardworking individuals. There's this feeling of understanding. I can see how Suit & Tie achieved everything he's accomplished (and I respect it). It's all he thinks about. It's all he talks about. Now that I think about it, the whole night we either talked about his crazy wild life or my crazy wild life. No "get to know" you questions. Another vodka cranberry later, we are making out in the streets.

**Takeaways**: I wake up the next morning excited to see Suit & Tie. Thursday is our planned dinner! No more unset schedules or last-minute plans. By 3:43 p.m., I hadn't heard from him, so I send him a text. He calls me right after to explain that he's unsure of how serious his meeting is and doesn't know what time he can meet me. He can hear the disappointment in my voice and asks if I'm upset.

If Suit & Tie likes me, why would he postpone our date? The moment he sends the text about meeting later, I send a text to my friends and make other plans. I knew he was going to cancel. I just knew it. And I wasn't going to "wait around" for him. I didn't hear from him until 9 p.m. He didn't cancel on me until 11 p.m., when I was out at Little Woodrow's, watching turtles race.

Clearly, Suit & Tie is focused on himself and what he wants. I'm not even sure why he asked me out on a second date if he never intended to pursue this seriously. At least cancel if you can't commit. I doubt there will be another date with Suit & Tie, and he doesn't seem interested anyway. Dating is a mutual decision, and it's as much my choice as it is the man's whether or not we want to see each other again. After two dates, I don't know enough about Suit & Tie to write him off, but I don't think dating a girl that lives in Houston is worth it to him.

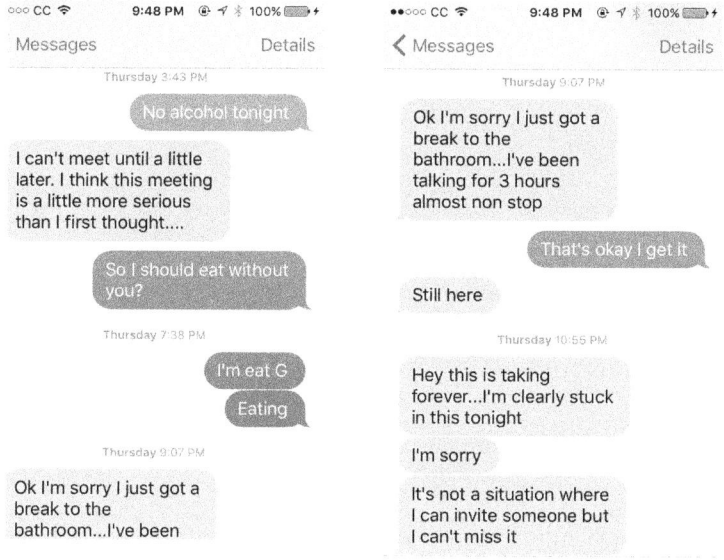

# DATE DIARY: TINTED OAKLEYS

May 27, 2016

**Date's Nickname**: Tinted Oakleys

**Age**: 26

**Occupation**: Consultant

**How We Met**: Coffee Meets Bagel. He messages me about Aka Sushi

**Where We Went**: Aka Sushi (this place is cursed)

**What I Ate**: Edamame and an avocado and cucumber Roll (I don't change)

**Total Cost Estimate**: –$10

**Prior Expectations**: I've been extremely picky on my dating apps lately, probably too picky. I like this guy's profile and go out of my way to "discover" him (it's the equivalent to a super like on Tinder). We set plans to meet at Aka Sushi because he lives across the street.

**Date Diary**: I'm already getting echo vibes from my date with Cheap Ass. I arrive before him and wait outside.

**First Thoughts**: He shows up wearing Tinted Oakleys (too Jersey Shore for my taste). Shorter than expected. I'm more into his profile pictures than his real life physical appearance.

The waitress leads us to a table located in the middle of the restaurant, which may or may not be the exact same table I sat at with Cheap Ass. Within the first five minutes of our date, Tinted Oakleys receives a phone call. He answers his phone and starts a conversation with his roommate, and tells him he's out to dinner "with a girl." Immediately after Tinted Oakleys hangs up, he turns to me, and says, "My roommate is giving me a hard time about answering the phone on a date. I didn't know if it was urgent or not, so I answered."

I'm rolling my eyes and out of force reply with an, "Understandable." To be honest, that statement is directed toward Tinted Oakleys' roommate being right about answering your phone during a date.

We start talking about where we grew up, what schools we attended, and our weekend plans. I like Tinted Oakleys, but I'm feeling a friend vibe by the time our food arrives. I'm having fun getting to know him though. He's still in the bachelor mindset and flies all over the country to visit his high school friends. We talk about places we've traveled and how good Aka Sushi's happy hour is. Thankfully, the dating app topic never comes up.

By the time the bill comes, Tinted Oakleys reaches for his wallet. There is no hesitation like with Cheap Ass. I know if I sit here in silence, Tinted Oakleys will pay for my food. I do offer, and he accepts. This time, I don't mind paying because there is no spark and I wouldn't go on a second date with Tinted Oakleys. After we pay, Tinted Oakleys and I walk out of the restaurant. We hug and exchange few words about how much fun we had and we'll talk soon.

**Takeaways**: I hope answering your phone during dinner and splitting checks isn't modern dating. It doesn't make a girl feel special. This date is so casual I could've been getting to know my coworkers, my second cousins, or random strangers on the street. I doubt either of us will reach out.

# DATE DIARY: CREEPY MF

May 28, 2016

**Date's Nickname**: Creepy MF

**Age**: 28

**Occupation**: Contractor

**How We Met**: Tinder

**Where We Went**: His apartment pool

**What I Ate**: Nothing

**Total Cost Estimate**: $0

**Prior Expectations**: The same day I match with Creepy MF is the same day I go on this date. He invites me to a pool party at his apartment pool for Memorial Day weekend. Meeting at a stranger's apartment complex is sketchy, but I figure it would be an interesting story and it's free.

**Date Diary**: I drove to Creepy MF's apartment on one stipulation. For no reason am I going to enter his apartment. Creepy MF meets me in the garage of his apartment building.

**First Thoughts**: He's older and balder than his profile pictures. No initial attraction at all. However, since I'm already here, I want to hang out and at least get to know him.

Immediately, Creepy MF walks me straight to his apartment, saying he needs a drink refill. Wary of my stipulation, I lurk outside the doorway. Creepy MF offers me a drink, which I decline. I close the door and wait in the hallway. 20 seconds later, Creepy MF leads me to the pool.

Creepy MF introduces me to a couple of his friends before we hop in the pool. For the most part, he seems normal. Creepy MF just moved into this apartment building and is making new friends. Creepy MF tells me about his struggles meeting people. He says when he goes out people tend to stay with their group. I agree and can relate. Most people don't mingle with strangers anymore; I may have tons of strangers asking me out via text message, but barely have any asking me out in person.

After an hour and a half, I'm ready to go. Creepy MF offers to walk me out. Creepy MF wants to "drop something off" before walking me to the garage. Replay first encounter. He opens the door, and I am still uncomfortable entering his apartment. Creepy MF can take a hint.

As soon as he puts his stuff down, he turns around and walks me to my car. We arrive, and Creepy MF asks what I'm doing later. I tell him that I made tentative plans to go out with some friends.

He responds, "Great, I think I'm going out too. I'll let you know where we go." We hug, and I get into my car.

**Takeaways**: That night, I get a couple of messages from Creepy MF notifying me of his whereabouts. I respond with a "Sorry, we ended up not going out tonight," which triggers a persistent exchange. NO MEANS NO, not "convince me". At that hour of night, I assume any man who wants to meet me just wants to have sex, and, if my goal was to have sex, it wouldn't be with an old, bald, creepy guy.

As soon as he sent me the final "Do you wanna meet up?" text message, I block his number.

# DATE DIARY: BORDERLINE RAPIST

May 29, 2016

**Date's Nickname**: Borderline Rapist

**Age**: 31

**Occupation**: Something at BHP

**How We Met**: Hinge

**Where We Went**: We were supposed to go to a bar and grab drinks

**What I Ate**: Nothing

**Total Cost Estimate**: $0

**Prior Expectations**: I receive a text from Borderline Rapist at 1 a.m. on Sunday night. I've talked with him a few times previously via text and phone call. He's very social and easy to talk to but never initiated a meet up until now. The past two nights, I've had boys texting me late at night

asking to meet up for what a girl can assume is a booty call. Immediately after Borderline Rapist's last pictured text, he calls me. Over the phone I tell Borderline Rapist that I'm uncomfortable meeting him for the first time at my house or his. He tells me he's had a bad night and just wants someone to talk to over drinks. Borderline Rapist then offers to pick me up on our way to the bar. Reluctantly, I agree.

**Date Diary**: Ten minutes later, a silver Mercedes pulls into my driveway.

**First Thoughts**: He looks exactly like his profile pictures: very fit and tan. Wearing basketball shorts and a tank. Drinking out of a protein shake bottle.

As he drives away from my house, Borderline Rapist says, "I need to stop by my house real quick to change clothes."

I'm already extremely uncomfortable and tell Borderline Rapist that I will wait in the car while he changes. Borderline Rapist pulls into his driveway and starts making small talk.

After five minutes he says, "The bars are closing soon anyways. We can grab a drink inside," then opens his door, and enters his house before I have time to respond.

This is where I should have put my foot down, said something, and gone home, but I didn't.

By the time I enter his house, Borderline Rapist can tell I'm uncomfortable, as I've verbally told him. I walk through his house trembling. He leads me to the kitchen and introduces me to his friend. Borderline Rapist and his friend start chatting about their evening events. From their conversation, I conclude Borderline Rapist and his friends were out at a club party. Borderline Rapist and his brother met these two girls, who they brought back to their house. Borderline Rapist's girl didn't tell Borderline Rapist she had a boyfriend until after she agreed to come over.

His girl ditches while her friend stays and hooks up with his brother. Apparently, the girl who left had been making out with Borderline Rapist all afternoon. My theory is that she didn't have a boyfriend; she probably used that as an excuse to get the hell out.

As Borderline Rapist and his friend relive the night, they constantly offer me alcohol. I decline, and they taunt me.

Borderline Rapist says, "Honestly, I'm surprised you're not more fun."

I'm trying to give Borderline Rapist the benefit of the doubt, despite having been manipulated into his house. I try to keep my actions, my words, and my body composed, but I'm fighting my survival instincts.

We sit on the couch and start talking. I can't remember what we talked about. I only remember thinking of ways to calm myself down. We're sitting on separate sides of the couch with no physical contact when Borderline Rapist says, "Come with me, I want to show you something." He leads to me his back patio, which has a small pool and hanging lights. He even has one of those swan inflatables. We walk back inside, and Borderline Rapist leads me to his bedroom.

Borderline Rapist hops on his bed and says, "Check out this pillow I just bought. It's the best pillow I've ever owned." I stand at the edge of the bed and don't say anything.

I'm not stupid; I know exactly what he is trying to do.

Borderline Rapist can take a hint. He looks at me and says, "Don't worry; we are not going to do anything you do not want to do."

I tend to take people at their word. I believe that most people are inherently good. I lower my guard. I decide to lie down on the bed.

I position myself far away and try to talk about anything else. Borderline Rapist starts putting on the moves.

He tells me I can get any guy I want, that my Facebook pictures don't do my beauty justice, and wants to introduce me to some of his friends "who I would love to date."

Then, the caressing starts. As we're talking, he tries to go in for a kiss.

I stop him and say, "I'm sorry but I do not want to hook up with you. We should just be friends."

Borderline Rapist responds, "I'm going to be 100% honest with you. I want to rip off all your clothes. I already have a lot of friends. So, what's in it for me?"

At this point I am only chatting about friendship to stall for an escape route. I have no intention of seeing Borderline Rapist ever again.

We talk some more before Borderline Rapist leaves the room, but not before he tells me to stay where I am. Borderline Rapist reenters the room and we chat about the many pictures he has of himself hanging from his wall… until he tries to pick me up and place me on his bed. He bends down, grabs my legs and lower back. I panic. I tell him to put me down, which he does, and that I'm ready to leave. His response, "You can Uber home, right?" I grab my purse and flee from his house.

I walk out front and try to order an Uber, but my phone is not in my purse. It has to be in his house. I ring the doorbell and wait outside for someone to answer. No one does. I wait around for about five minutes before I decide on Plan B: I only live a mile from this house and can walk home at 3:30 a.m. all by myself with no phone and no form of protection. Reality sinks in as I get closer to my house. How did I get myself into this situation? Why did I get into a car with a man I never met? Why am I walking home by myself at 3:30 a.m.?

**Takeaways**: That night, I sob in bed unable to sleep. I've never felt more unsafe or uneasy, and the thought of returning to his house for my phone and seeing him again sickens me. Every imaginable circumstance of what could've happened plays in my mind. In the morning, I contact a few friends via Facebook. I cannot go back to that house by myself. By 10 a.m., I have no leads. I realize I have a date scheduled at 11 a.m. and no way to contact my date. I hate cancelled plans and no shows. I arrive at the planned location only to find a closed restaurant (it's Memorial Day). I'm so distraught by the past 12 hours. I need to tell someone. I drive to a friend's apartment and unload everything on him.

By 1 p.m. I receive Borderline Rapist's brother's contact information. My friend does all the work from this point forward. My friend texts Borderline Rapist's brother asking for my phone. He drives to Borderline Rapist's house and picks up my phone. He takes me to eat and tries to calm me down. I look at my phone and receive this message from the guy I stood up. I can't believe I stood someone up. That's not who I am.

Did Borderline Rapist do anything illegal? No. Did Borderline Rapist lie to me about going to a bar, offer me alcohol, make fun of me for not taking it, tell me he was not going to do anything, hear me reject a each of his advances and still try to persuade me to sleep with him? Yes. Did he value me as more than an object to fill his need? No. He didn't have the decency to take me home (or even make sure I got an Uber) or answer the door at 3:30 a.m.

The only thing that separates him from a rapist is the physical act. Why did he think disturbing persistence would change my mind? I am not game. I NEVER want my friends or any girl to feel the way Borderline Rapist made me feel that night: that my only purpose is to fulfill HIS need.

# DATE DIARY: DJ BLENZ

May 31, 2016

**Date's Nickname**: DJ Blenz

**Age**: 33

**Occupation**: Radio DJ

**How We Met**: The producer from the morning radio show set us up.

**Where We Went**: Dinner and Drinks–The Flat, a nightspot and lounge

**What I ate**: Veggie pizza, cocktails, and a frozen mojito

**Total Cost Estimate**: $75

**Prior Expectations**: This is my last date of No Pay May. After what happened Sunday night, I need my final date to be fun and original! I plan everything. I want to spend the last day of May listening to the soft, smooth stylings of jazz (channeling my inner Billie Holiday). I send DJ Blenz this promo poster for the The Flat's Jazz Jam and ask him to meet me there at 7:30 p.m.

**Date Diary**: I arrive before DJ Blenz and sit myself at the empty bar. I'm chatting with the bartender as DJ Blenz walks in.

**First Thoughts**: He's good looking and definitely looks like a DJ. Nose ring. Tattoos. He grooms his hair well. Not normally the type of guy I go for.

This is a blind date for DJ Blenz. He doesn't know my real name until we introduce ourselves at the bar. DJ Blenz obviously knows about *No Pay May*, so it's a no-pressure date, and the only thing he's worried about it what nickname he will earn. In reality, all I'm trying to do on this date is get drunk and listen to a few horn solos, and it seems like DJ Blenz is game.

I'm pleasantly surprised that it doesn't take long for us to start cracking jokes and throwing subtle sarcasm. I start with a specialty cocktail. I'm not expecting DJ Blenz to pay, but he does. I learn that DJ Blenz just moved to Houston from Las Vegas. He doesn't tell me much about his time in Vegas; what happens in Vegas stays in Vegas. However, DJ Blenz explains how he ended up on the radio.

It's late, and I haven't eaten. The bar only serves pizza (at least it's not steak). I order a veggie pizza and tell DJ Blenz that I'll pay for it. The jazz band shows up, along with a sea of interesting individuals. Apparently Jazz Jam doesn't start until after 9 p.m., despite the advertised time on the promo graphic.

DJ Blenz gets the second round, and the first set plays without any horns. No horns in a jazz band? Unacceptable. Thankfully, the crowd keeps us entertained. We're an eclectic bunch: a guy sitting on the couch reading a book, a couple's make-out corner, a dude dancing like he can't control his limbs, and us (a blind first date setup through a radio station).

I'm having a great time with DJ Blenz. I think we'd be great friends. The horn players show up when I'm three drinks in. Now the party has started! It's 10:30 p.m. when

DJ Blenz and I decide it's time to head out, but I could stay all night. I know I won't be going out on a Tuesday anytime in the near future. Cathy needs a break.

We walk outside and exchange a few words partnered with a hug.

**Takeaways**: This is the perfect way to end *No Pay May*. I spent my evening having fun, doing something different, and making a new friend. I really enjoyed my night! The next morning, I listen to DJ Blenz give his own version of my date diary on the local radio show. It seems that he also enjoyed our evening together.

# Epliogue

# DATE DIARY RECAP

June 1, 2016

Date's Nickname:

- Quiet but not Shy
- Over Talker
- Cynical Dater
- The Transient
- Preppy Texter
- Too Good to be True
- PFG & Short Shorts
- Brunch Enthusiast
- Perfect Dater
- Metro Man
- Cheap Ass
- Foul Mouth
- Derby Dude
- Adjuster
- Hint Dropper
- Future Boyfriend
- Brussels Sprouts
- Sweet Intentions
- Bird Poop
- Suit & Tie
- Big Personality
- Banana Republic
- Anal Bandit
- Donut Hole
- Kiss Cam
- Tinted Oakleys
- Creepy MF
- Borderline Rapist
- DJ Blenz

Dang. 29 different men. 29 first dates. 2 second dates. I made a bracket.

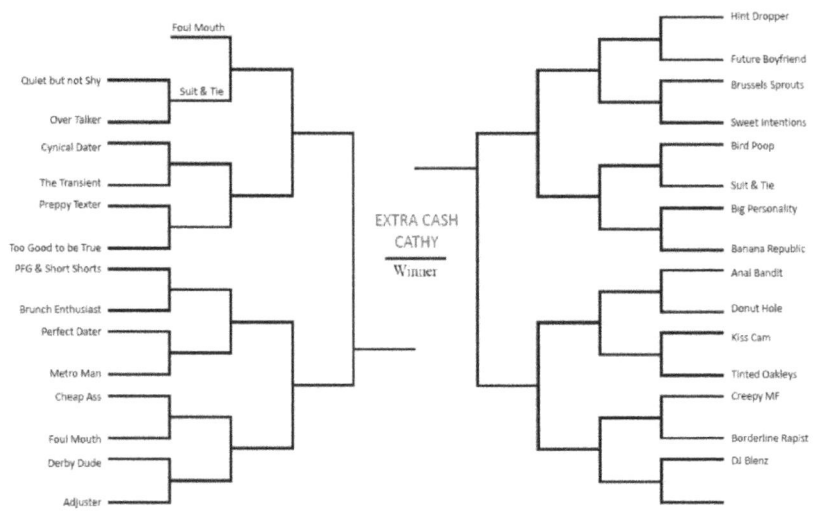

Ages: 21–33 years old (12-year age range). I broke a few rules.

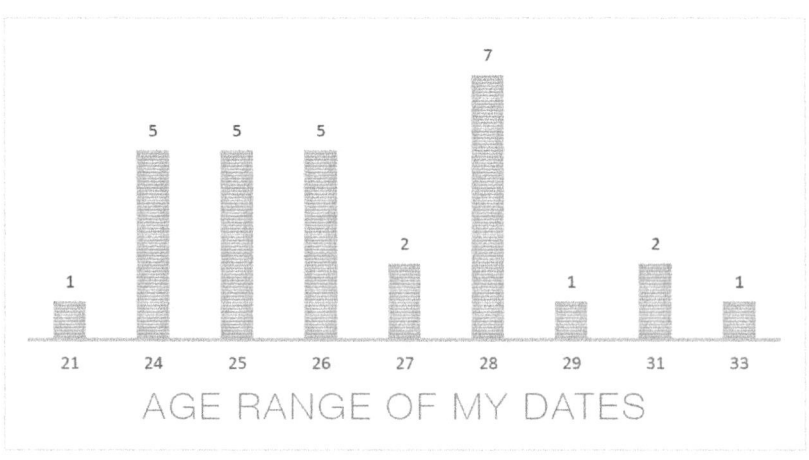

Occupation:

- Doctor
- Med School Resident
- Freelancer
- Sales Manager
- Lawyer
- IT Analyst
- Investment Banker
- Engineer
- Engineer
- Engineer
- Engineer
- Navy Seal
- Engineer
- Private Investigator
- Grad student
- IT Analyst
- Engineer
- Engineer
- Engineer
- CEO
- Financial Advisor
- Engineer
- Biochemist
- Abercrombie & Fitch Manager
- College student
- Consultant
- Contractor
- BHP
- Radio DJ

What can I say… Engineers Pay May!

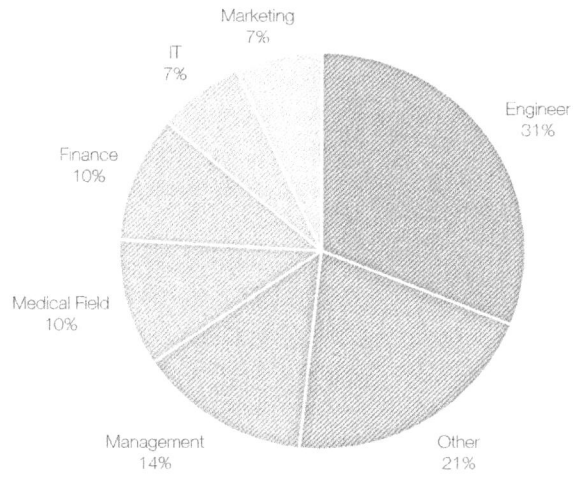

PROFESSIONS OF MY DATES

How We Met: Met up with dates from 5 of the 7 apps I downloaded during the month.

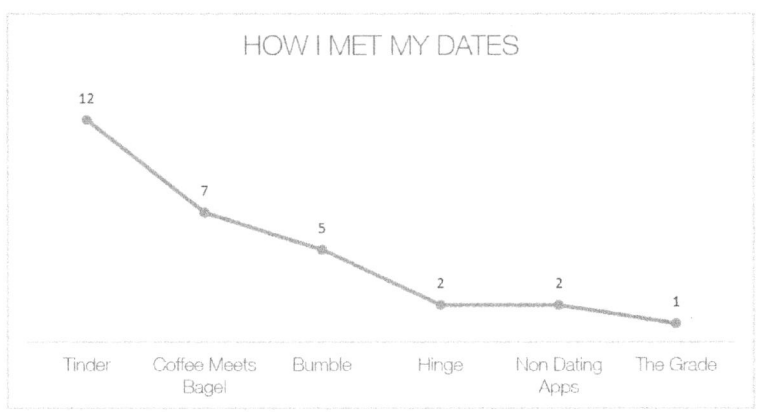

Where We Went:

| | |
|---|---|
| Batanga | An Art Festival |
| Fadi's | Liberty Kitchen |
| Aka Sushi | Gloria's |
| Local Foods | Lowbrow's |
| Axelrad | Aka Sushi |
| Tsukiji Sushi | Bollo |
| Derby Party | La Grange |
| Axelrad | Inversion Coffee |
| Axelrad | Union Kitchen |
| Porch Swing Pub | Astro's Game |
| Benjy's | Bovine & Barley |
| Izakaya | Aka Sushi |
| Onion Creek | A Pool |
| Oporto | My Date's House |
| Urban Eats | The Flat |

15 of these places I had never been before!

What I Ate:

| | |
|---|---|
| Tapas | Veggie Pizza |
| Falafel Platter | Veggie Pizza |
| Avocado Roll | Brussels Sprouts |
| Falafel Sandwich | Tapas |
| Veggie Pizza | Fried Pickles |
| Avocado Roll | Charred Veggies |
| Cheese Omelet | Cauliflower |
| Migas | Breakfast Taco |
| Veggie Sides | Margherita Pizza |
| Avocado Rolls | Tater Tots |
| Veggie Pizza | Avocado Roll |
| Caprese Salad | Veggie Pizza |

| % of Consumption over 31 Dates | |
|---|---|
| Alcohol | 65% |
| Plated Dinners | 29% |
| Pizza | 19% |
| Sushi | 13% |
| Brunch | 10% |
| Fried Food | 6% |

Total Cost Estimate:   $642 − $20 = $622

I turned a good profit. Men paid on 26 of my 31 dates. Three of my "dates" involved no money, and I paid for myself on two of my dates.

Prior Expectations: After reviewing my blog entries, I divided my prior expectations into three categories: excited, indifferent, and not excited.

- Excited: 14
- Indifferent: 14
- Not Excited: 3

Date Diary: Here a few behavioral trends.

- 8 of my 31 dates involved men driving me somewhere
- 7 of my 31 dates involved physical touch (I'm not talking about hugging)
- 6 of my 31 dates involved kissing

Takeaways: The odds are NOT in my favor.

- 14 of the 29 men never texted me after our first date.
- 9 of the 29 men texted me after our date but never initiated plans.
- 4 of the 29 men offered a second date, but I turned them down.
- 2 of the 29 men got a second date.

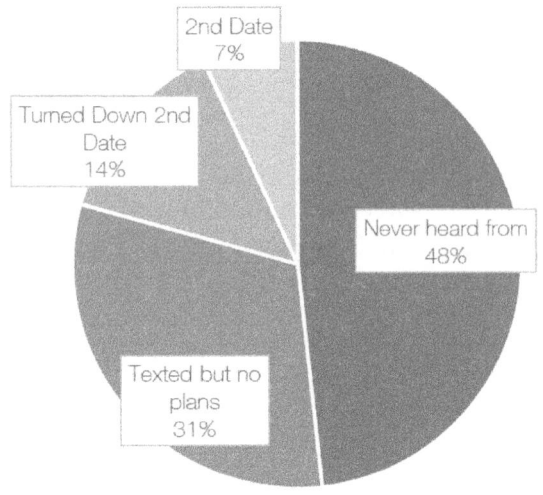

# THE END OF NO PAY MAY

June 2, 2016

*No Pay May* started as nothing more than a challenge. Can I do it? Can it be done? After voyaging through the entirety of this book, here's the short answer: YES.

    To all the guys of *No Pay May*, thank you! Thank you for dating me. Thank you, most of you, for spending your money on me. Thank you for teaching me. Thank you for giving me memories I'll never forget. I am sincerely grateful.

    I started *No Pay May* as an open-minded girl. All of my initial dates were new experiences. Before *No Pay May*... I never downloaded a dating app. I never messaged strangers. I never met up with strangers. I never went on a date with someone I had never met in person. It was all new. By the end of *No Pay May*, dates blurred together in routine monotony, and I became a cynical dater. Due to my unsustainable pace of dating so many people within a short amount of time, I picked up on a few trends.

    In general, I believe most men date with a purpose, usually either sex or serious relationship/marriage. After the first or second date, men tend to make a decision about whether a woman will potentially fill the desired purpose. I believe most women date to get to know someone, with the potential but not the preordained assumption of sex and/or a relationship. It takes time to build trust and understanding. Online dating, despite its convenience, did not make romance any easier. In a message-first, meet-later world, the uneasiness of a first date escalated as I began questioning:

Is this person a catfish or do they look like their profile picture? Are they on this dating app just to have sex? At the same time, the process of online dating provided me with boundless options. I started viewing people as numbers and profiles rather than individuals and, with every swipe, I became more and more shallow. By the end of May, I'd immediately swipe left if a guy was shorter than 6'1". Is that wrong? Did I miss out on a few great guys? Probably, but there were plenty of other candidates who met my requirement, and I didn't have time to message and meet everyone. Rather than expanding my horizons, online dating made me pickier, more impatient, and close-minded.

**Last Thoughts**: We all choose who we date and have our OWN opinions on dating. Are my opinions right? That's 100% debatable. Any regrets? Absolutely not! Even if I did gain five pounds and still didn't get a boyfriend–worth it!

**Takeaways**: *No Pay May* ended as more than a challenge. It's pure entertainment. It's a social dating experiment. I've told several of the men about *No Pay May* since it went public. And guess what? They don't really care that I wrote about our date. Most of them don't want the attention it brings, and the others never intended on asking me out again anyways. If you're worried about my dating life post *No Pay May*, you shouldn't be. Apparently, there are many men who still want a shot at love. Some are even amused enough by my experiences to take a serious interest (i.e. the following text thread).

# No Pay May | 167

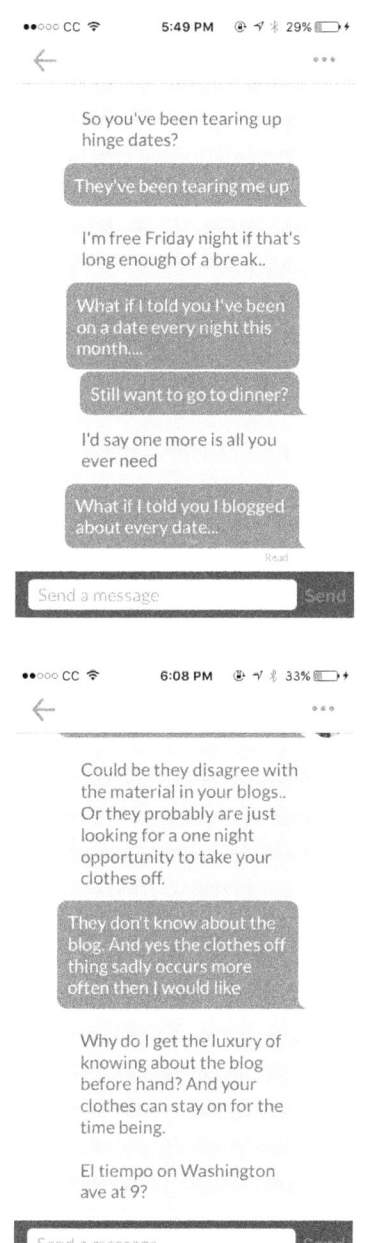

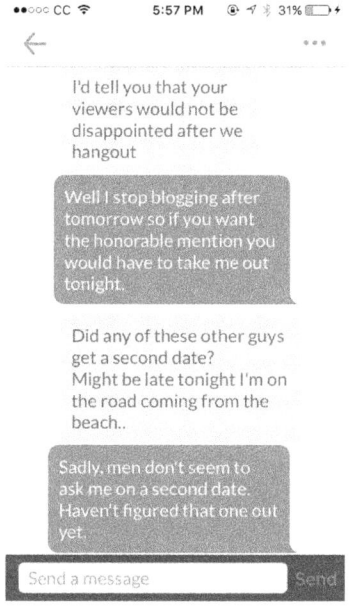

Have I become Houston's unofficial most eligible Bachelorette?

Humbly, I accept.

# The End.

APPENDIX

Date Outfits

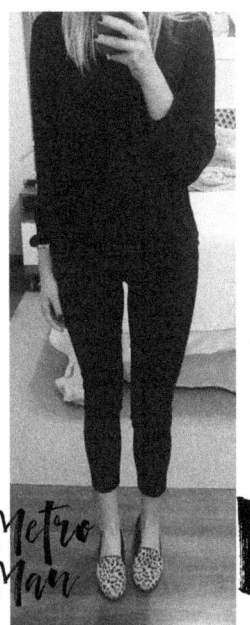
Metro Man

Kiss Cam

Creepy MF

DJ Bleuz

Cheap Ass

Brussels Sprouts

CPSIA information can be obtained
at www.ICGtesting.com
Printed in the USA
BVHW03s1746010518
514956BV00008B/222/P